Foundations and Opportunities of Biometrics

An Introduction to Technology, Applications, and Responsibilities

Dario Salice
Jennifer Salice

Apress®

Foundations and Opportunities of Biometrics: An Introduction to Technology, Applications, and Responsibilities

Dario Salice
Epsom, UK

Jennifer Salice
Epsom, UK

ISBN-13 (pbk): 979-8-8688-0508-0
https://doi.org/10.1007/979-8-8688-0509-7

ISBN-13 (electronic): 979-8-8688-0509-7

Copyright © 2024 by Dario Salice and Jennifer Salice

This work is subject to copyright. All rights are reserved by the Publisher, whether the whole or part of the material is concerned, specifically the rights of translation, reprinting, reuse of illustrations, recitation, broadcasting, reproduction on microfilms or in any other physical way, and transmission or information storage and retrieval, electronic adaptation, computer software, or by similar or dissimilar methodology now known or hereafter developed.

Trademarked names, logos, and images may appear in this book. Rather than use a trademark symbol with every occurrence of a trademarked name, logo, or image we use the names, logos, and images only in an editorial fashion and to the benefit of the trademark owner, with no intention of infringement of the trademark.

The use in this publication of trade names, trademarks, service marks, and similar terms, even if they are not identified as such, is not to be taken as an expression of opinion as to whether or not they are subject to proprietary rights.

While the advice and information in this book are believed to be true and accurate at the date of publication, neither the authors nor the editors nor the publisher can accept any legal responsibility for any errors or omissions that may be made. The publisher makes no warranty, express or implied, with respect to the material contained herein.

Managing Director, Apress Media LLC: Welmoed Spahr
Acquisitions Editor: Susan McDermott
Development Editor: Laura Berendson
Project Manager: Jessica Vakili

Cover image by Freepik (www.freepik.com)

Distributed to the book trade worldwide by Springer Science+Business Media New York, 1 NY Plaza, New York, NY 10004. Phone 1-800-SPRINGER, fax (201) 348-4505, e-mail orders-ny@springer-sbm.com, or visit www.springeronline.com. Apress Media, LLC is a California LLC and the sole member (owner) is Springer Science + Business Media Finance Inc (SSBM Finance Inc). SSBM Finance Inc is a **Delaware** corporation.

For information on translations, please e-mail booktranslations@springernature.com; for reprint, paperback, or audio rights, please e-mail bookpermissions@springernature.com.

Apress titles may be purchased in bulk for academic, corporate, or promotional use. eBook versions and licenses are also available for most titles. For more information, reference our Print and eBook Bulk Sales web page at http://www.apress.com/bulk-sales.

Any source code or other supplementary material referenced by the author in this book is available to readers on GitHub via the book's product page, located at www.apress.com/979-8-8688-0508-0. For more detailed information, please visit https://www.apress.com/gp/services/source-code.

If disposing of this product, please recycle the paper

For our daughter, Anna.

Table of Contents

About the Authors xiii
About the Technical Reviewer xv
Acknowledgments xvii
Introduction xix

Part I: Laying the Foundation 1

Chapter 1: The Growing Use of Biometrics 3
Biometrics in Film and Literature 3
    Fingerprint Analysis 4
    Facial Recognition 4
    Voice Identification and Analysis 5
    Iris and Retina Scan 5
First Uses of Biometrics 6
    Early Historical Use 6
    Use in Recent History 7
Biometrics in Our Lives Today 10
    Where We Encounter Biometrics 11
    Cameras in Public Spaces 12
    Personal Devices 14
    Biometrics at Home 15

TABLE OF CONTENTS

How Biometrics Became So Ubiquitous 17
    It Starts with the Sensors 17
    Processing Power Is More Readily Available 18
    Bandwidth and Connectivity 18
Summary 19

Chapter 2: What Are Biometrics? 21
What Is Biometric Data? 21
Traits and Features 22
What Is Biometric Data Used For? 23
    Types of Problems Solved Using Biometrics 23
    Identifying the Problem Being Addressed 30
The Journey of Biometric Data 31
    Signal Acquisition (Collection) 31
    Signal Processing and Feature Extraction 32
    Data Storage 33
    Comparison and Matching 33
    Decision-Making 35
    Action 35
    Adaption 35
Summary 36

Chapter 3: Adversarial Behavior—Attack and Defense 37
Attacks—Bad Actions 37
    Make Bad Actions More Expensive 38
    General Types of Attacks 39
    Artificial Intelligence (AI) to Attack Biometrics 40
Examples of Attacks Against Biometrics 41
    Stolen Biometric Data 41

Artificially Created Information 42
   Potential Future Threats 42
  Defense 43
   Layered Approach 43
   Liveness 43
   The Utopia to Keep Biometrics Secret 45
   Goal to Check for Liveness 46
   Active Liveness 48
   Passive Liveness 49
  Summary 50

Part II: Sources of Biometric Signals 51

Chapter 4: Physiological Characteristics 53

  Fingerprints 53
   What Are They? 54
   What Are Some Benefits and Drawbacks of Using Fingerprints? 54
   In What Contexts Are They Used? 56
   How Does It Work? 57
   Interesting Details About Fingerprints 58
  Iris 59
   What Are They? 59
   In What Contexts Are They Used? 60
   How Does It Work? 60
   Interesting Details About Irises 61
  Retina 61
   What Are They? 61
   In What Contexts Are They Used? 63
   How Does It Work? 63

TABLE OF CONTENTS

DNA 63
    What Is It? 64
    In What Contexts Is It Used? 64
    How Does It Work? 65
    Interesting Details About DNA 65
Summary 66

Chapter 5: Variable Human Characteristics—Face 67
What Characteristics Make the Face a Suitable Biometric Trait? 67
In What Contexts Are They Used? 68
How Does It Work? 70
Strengths and Weaknesses of Facial biometrics 72
    Strengths of Facial Biometrics 72
    Weaknesses of Facial Biometrics 73
Search Engines for Faces 74
    Face Search for Law Enforcement 75
    Face Search for Consumers 75
    Accuracy and False Positives 76
    Good Intentions 77
Summary 77

Chapter 6: Behavioral Characteristics 79
Typing Patterns 80
    How Does It Work? 81
    In What Contexts Are They Used? 81
    Limitations 82
    Privacy and Legal Risks 83
Walking Patterns/Gait Recognition 84

TABLE OF CONTENTS

    How Does It Work? 85
    Limitations 86
    In What Contexts Are They Used? 87
  Other Movement and Behavior 88
    Detection of Device Possession Change 89
    Prevalence of Use 90
  Summary 91

Chapter 7: Voice **93**
  What Characteristics Make Voice a Suitable Biometric Trait? 94
  How Voice Is Captured 95
  Strengths and Weaknesses 95
    Strengths 96
    Weaknesses 96
  In What Contexts Are They Used? 97
  Smart Speakers 100
  Environmental Factors 102
  How Does the Aging Voice Impact Its Use as a Biometric Signal? 103
  Risks and Attack Methods 104
  Summary 105

Part III: Critical Analysis **107**

Chapter 8: How Do We Judge Accuracy? **109**
  What Does It Mean to Be Correct? 109
  What Is an Error? 112
    Sensitivity 113
    Specificity 114
    Type I and Type II Errors 114

TABLE OF CONTENTS

Performance of Various Methods 116
    The Layers of Quality 117
    The Difficulty of Comparing Biometrics 117
    Fingerprint 118
    Voice Recognition 119
    Facial Recognition 120
Summary 121

Chapter 9: Challenges and Responsibilities 123

Matching of Biometrics Is Probabilistic in Nature 124
Consequences of Errors 124
    Identify the Risk of Getting It Wrong 126
Are Biometrics the End of Privacy? 127
    It Depends 128
    Common Concerns About Privacy 129
    Situational Compartmentalization 130
Racial Bias in Biometrics 131
    It's Not Just the Technology 132
    Lack of Diversity in Training Data 133
    Consent to Collect Biometric Data for Training Purposes 134
Accessibility 135
Risks of Collecting and Storing Data 136
Responsibilities 137
    Gather Informed Consent and Provide Transparency 138
    Prioritize Data Security and Privacy 138
    Ensure Accuracy 139
    Limit to Ethically Defensible Use 139
    Compliance and Legal Considerations 139

Accountability and User Education 140
Summary.. 140

Chapter 10: Usability and Practicality 141
How Usable Is the Product? 141
    Availability: Do People Have Access to the Technology They Need?............ 142
    Practicality.. 145
    Environment 145
    Usability.. 148
Intent.. 151
    Showing and Detecting Intent 151
    Difficulty of Showing and Assessing Intent 153
    Lack of Intent.. 155
    Reasonable Expectations 156
Summary.. 158

Conclusion 159

Index 163

About the Authors

Dario Salice is a technologist with over 20 years of experience in a broad range of roles. Originally from Switzerland, he spent time living and working in Silicon Valley before moving to the United Kingdom. His previous employers include Swisscom, Google, and Facebook/Meta, where he held roles around product management and cybersecurity. Dario represented Facebook/Meta on the board of the FIDO Alliance—an industry standardization body for authentication. Currently working as a freelance technologist, Dario consults with organizations on product development and cybersecurity.

Jennifer Salice is a veteran mathematics teacher with a passion for curriculum writing and teaching calculus. Her other professional interests include neurodiversity with an emphasis on autism and PDA. Originally from Atlanta, Jennifer has also lived in Jamaica, Spain, and California. She currently lives in the UK working on various projects from home.

About the Technical Reviewer

Massimo Nardone has more than 22 years of experience in security, web and mobile development, cloud, and IT architecture. His true IT passions are security and Android. He has been programming and teaching how to program with Android, Perl, PHP, Java, VB, Python, C/C++, and MySQL for more than 20 years. Massimo also holds a Master of Science degree in computing science from the University of Salerno, Italy. He has worked as a project manager, software engineer, research engineer, chief security architect, information security manager, PCI/SCADA auditor, and senior lead IT security/cloud/SCADA architect for many years. His technical skills include security, Android, cloud, Java, MySQL, Drupal, Cobol, Perl, web and mobile development, MongoDB, D3, Joomla, Couchbase, C/C++, WebGL, Python, Pro Rails, Django CMS, Jekyll, Scratch, etc. Massimo currently works as Chief Information Security Officer (CISO) for Cargotec Oyj. He worked as visiting lecturer and supervisor for exercises at the Networking Laboratory of the Helsinki University of Technology (Aalto University). He holds four international patents (PKI, SIP, SAML, and proxy areas).

Acknowledgments

It's been a great adventure writing this book. We'd like to thank the whole team at Apress for their trust and support.

There are numerous people who read through drafts of chapters and gave us feedback. We've enjoyed all the conversations—some resulting in us adding content and others leading us to remove content and stay focused.

Thanks to the following people for the feedback and contributions:

- Abishek Gupta
- Andreas Schmid
- Manish Gupta
- Luca Baronti
- Armaan Shahanshah
- Manos Mavrikos (FaceTec)
- Nicholas Cariello
- Paolo Gasti

Kristen Wallerius who took our initial idea and provided targeted nudges deserves an honorable mention here, as do all our friends and family who listened to us talking about it for the past year and a half.

Introduction

Your phone scans your face to give you access. Your laptop uses your fingerprint. Your smart speaker recognizes your voices and answers questions based on which user asked them. These are just a few of the ways biometric data is used in our everyday lives. In your personal and professional life, you might encounter situations where a good understanding of biometrics smoothes communication and helps create shared understanding with your peers.

The idea of writing this book came a few years ago when Dario began teaching an introductory module about Biometrics at HWZ in Switzerland. The module was part of a larger course titled "Disruptive Technologies," in which professionals in non-technical roles learned about the basics of disruptive technologies.

Welcome to this book about biometric data. The purpose of this book is to provide you with a foundational understanding of what biometrics are, what they're used for, how they work, and the limitations and responsibilities of using them. We hope that it will give you insights you expected and surprise you in other ways. We wanted to create a foundational book to help readers connect the dots between buzzwords, technology, risks, and opportunities. We hope this book proves useful in providing you with a solid overview of the topic.

Visit biometrics.jenario.com for information about this.

PART I

Laying the Foundation

CHAPTER 1

The Growing Use of Biometrics

> **Did you know?** If you visit someone or deliver to a US home, there's a 16%[1] chance that your face will be detected and analyzed by a video-enabled doorbell.

The use of biometrics in our lives is increasing exponentially. For the vast majority of us, our biometric data is being used multiple times each day. In this chapter, we will look at the path biometrics has taken through science fiction and historical use to bring us to our current-day experience with biometric data.

Biometrics in Film and Literature

Long before we could open our phones by scanning our face, we dreamed of the possibilities our particular body signals might unlock. As with many other technologies and innovations, the idea of using human characteristics to solve problems of security, access, and a host of others

---

[1] Prevalence of video-enabled doorbell cameras in the US: www.telecompetitor.com/video-doorbell-research-amazon-ring-tops-in-market-share-with-16-of-households-opting-in.

© Dario Salice and Jennifer Salice 2024
D. Salice and J. Salice, *Foundations and Opportunities of Biometrics*,
https://doi.org/10.1007/979-8-8688-0509-7_1

has long tugged on the collective imagination. In literature as well as film, popular culture often proves to be leading the way toward technological innovations. Often decades ahead of reality, what we can only conceive of in our imaginations makes its way into fictional works. Science fiction can show us what new technologies may look like and how they might be used in day-to-day tasks.

It's easy enough to do a quick search and find numerous examples of biometrics being used ahead of their time in movies, television, and literature. To prime your imagination for what's to come, we'll go over a select few before moving along the timeline toward actual present-day use.

Fingerprint Analysis

As early as the late 1800s, Arthur Conan Doyle wrote examples of his character Sherlock Holmes using fingerprints to identify criminals. While a small number of police agencies around the world were beginning to utilize this method, it was far from commonplace.

Fast forward about a century and we find some more technology-supported examples of fingerprint analysis in the movie *Back to the Future 2*. In one scene, Marty McFly opens the doors of the DeLorean using his fingerprint. In another scene, Doc Brown uses his thumbprint to confirm payment after being dropped off by a taxi. Here we see not only the introduction of a computer-based technology, but also uses of fingerprints outside the context of crime-solving.

Facial Recognition

An early example of the use of technology to aid in facial recognition can be seen in a 1966 television episode. Batman and Robin used their "Batphotoscope" to access a picture of a suspect they saw on the TV in their Batmobile. The Batmobile could receive an image of the suspect found in a database from the central 'bat cave computer' and print it out so

CHAPTER 1   THE GROWING USE OF BIOMETRICS

Batman could use his marker to reproduce the facial hair and mask of the villain. Given the low resolution on the Batmobile's screen, the confidence in the result might be questionable.

As with the Sherlock Holmes example, in this case the actual analysis is not carried out using technology. Nonetheless, the move toward seeing technology as an invaluable tool in solving crimes is well under way.

Many later movies such as *Robocop*, *The Fifth Element*, and *Terminator* use the idea of facial recognition either to provide access to a building or a vehicle or to recognize a face from a database of known individuals.

Voice Identification and Analysis

Similarly to facial recognition, voice as a biometric signal has long been used in science fiction. In films such as *Demolition Man*, the voice is used to identify an individual requesting access to a restricted space. On television's *Knight Rider*, Kit—the car—always correctly understood Michael Knight's instructions. It's interesting to note the ways our current-day voice assistants are still struggling with this.

Iris and Retina Scan

In the first installment of the *Mission Impossible* movie series, a CIA analyst called William Donloe is seen using a retina scanner in order to infiltrate a vault where Ethan Hunt is hanging upside down. This identification process is not clearly shown, but the use of a specialized scanner mounted next to the entrance of the vault is implied.

In the James Bond movie *Never Say Never Again* we see an example of a character bypassing a sophisticated biometric authentication method. Jack Petachi, an Air Force pilot forced to work for SPECTRE, tricked the biometric authentication system into identifying him as the president. He did this by connecting a portable electronic eye-scanning system to the central control unit. In order to impersonate the president of the United States for

5

retina-based authentication, he removed the front of a robotic eye exposing electronics that successfully mimicked the president's eyes. In this way, he was able to access and activate a missile system.

In these examples, and many more, we see humanity's fascination with the possibilities held within our personal human data. We are always seeking more sophisticated ways to identify, authenticate, and control access. Writers create curious and compelling scenarios which draw in an audience eager to envision what the future may hold. In more ways than the writers might have predicted, the situation presented in science fiction and crime stories continue to make their way into our real-life experiences.

First Uses of Biometrics

In this section, we will look at the development of biometrics throughout history. As with the previous section, we will present a select group of examples to paint a picture, rather than attempt to list out each use of biometrics throughout history.

Early Historical Use

Humans have been walking around with unique fingerprints, retinas, facial features, and vital signs for millennia. Although we've only been automating the use of these signals over the past several decades, people have been using them in more analog ways for much, much longer.

One of the first instances of physical characteristics being recorded and used to identify people was about 3,500 years ago during the Babylonian[2] times. The height of a suspected or convicted criminal was recorded and used as a means of identification. Fingerprints were also used on clay tablets, along with other inscriptions, for the purpose of record keeping.

---

[2] https://recfaces.com/articles/history-of-biometrics.

CHAPTER 1   THE GROWING USE OF BIOMETRICS

Aside from the Babylonians, there is also historical record from China,[3] more than 2,000 years ago, of handprints being used as a means of identification for legal documents. It is not known if the uniqueness of fingerprints was wholly understood at that time, but they were treated as one data point that would aid in the verification of the author of a document. In some places (like India[4]) a fingerprint can still be a valid form of signature for people who are illiterate, infants, or for other reasons unable to sign using their name. In these cases, males are told to use their left hand thumb and females the right hand thumb.

Use in Recent History

Can you remember?   The first time you encountered a new use of biometrics in your life? *I remember the first time I set up voice recognition to access a financial account by phone. I was recently surprised to find that, 15 years later, the same phrase with my significantly older voice, can still be used to help me gain access to this account.*

With technological innovations and advancements, the first uses are usually restricted to highly specialized areas. There can be various reasons for this. Initially, access to a new technology is cost-prohibitive for wider use. As the technology improves over time, it can be expected to become more cost-efficient to produce in mass. It is only at this point that the larger part of the population gains access to the innovation.

---

[3] China: early use of biometrics 1-8 www.ojp.gov/pdffiles1/nij/225321.pdf.
[4] fingerprint as a signature www.eoiburkinafaso.gov.in/page/general-guidelines-for-passport-and-consular-services/#:~:text=Those%20who%20cannot%20affix%20their,use%20right%20hand%20thumb%20impression.

CHAPTER 1   THE GROWING USE OF BIOMETRICS

Aside from cost, by definition, innovation is driven by new thoughts and ideas that are not commonly understood or accepted. The usual path of innovation is from a small group of people implementing a new idea until it can be improved and shown to be useful for society as a whole. In the following sections, we'll go through a select timeline of the emergence of new techniques that in modern day use are more accessible.

1850: What is considered to be the first systematic approach to collecting and storing fingerprints was invented by an employee of India's Civil Service organization. Sir William Hershell recorded the handprints[5] of employees on the back of their contract in order to identify them at pay day.

1870: An approach to using a combination of biometric data such as height, weight, size of the head, arms, and feet to identify criminals was first used in France in 1879. The system[6] of anthropometry, measurement of body characteristics, was widely used by police organizations across the world and regarded as the gold standard until the early 20th century. Although the system did help law enforcement identify criminals, it would soon become clear that the characteristics weren't unique enough to ensure reliable identification.

1903: At the start of the 20th century, the New York Civil Service Commission started collecting the fingerprints of their applicants to prevent test fraud during the recruiting process. Shortly after that, the New York State Prison system started using this practice to identify criminals.

1904: The first fingerprint bureaus to systematically collect and store fingerprints[7] of known criminals were opened in the St Louis police departments and the US penitentiary in Kansas.

---

[5] https://recfaces.com/articles/history-of-biometrics.
[6] www.thalesgroup.com/en/markets/digital-identity-and-security/government/inspired/history-of-biometric-authentication.
[7] https://recfaces.com/articles/history-of-biometrics.

CHAPTER 1   THE GROWING USE OF BIOMETRICS

1970s: Various efforts were made to automate the collection of fingerprints and other unique human characteristics like images of the iris. This was in an effort to reduce the workload and cost of collecting data for the purpose of identifying criminals. The first automated fingerprint identification system (AFIS)[8] was introduced by the FBI in 1974. Due to the high cost of storing digital information, the system would only store the most important elements of the fingerprint. Automation would allow police officers to compare a given fingerprint with 100,000 stored prints in just under 30 minutes. Before these room-sized computers were available, such an endeavor would take at least a month. Finding the advancement highly valuable, the FBI subsequently accelerated the availability of these readers by funding their continued development and manufacture.

1996: To provide secure access to the Olympic Village during the Olympic Games in Atlanta,[9] a hand geometry system was deployed. More than 65,000 people were enrolled and it processed more than one million requests during the four weeks the Olympic Games took place. Although it was a large-scale deployment, it is still very narrow compared to what would come in the early 2000s.

2001: Technological advancements were rapid but certainly not linear. A face-recognition system deployed for the Super Bowl in Tampa, Florida delivered mixed results. Out of 100,000 spectators, the local police department identified 19 people with criminal records.[10] This process garnered a lot of criticism due to the fact that all 19 individuals had been

---

[8] www.innovatrics.com/glossary/afis-automated-fingerprint-identification-system.

[9] Olympics Atlanta—www.biometricupdate.com/201802/history-of-biometrics-2#:~:text=A%20major%20public%20use%20of,enrollment%20of%20over%2065%2C000%20people.

[10] www.wired.com/2002/12/biometrics-benched-for-super-bowl/.

charged with only petty[11] crimes. This case can provide the basis for a debate on individual privacy vs. group security.

2013: The introduction of a fingerprint sensor in the iPhone 5s[12] can be considered another milestone where more people started to have access to a consumer grade device with biometric capabilities.

2015: Microsoft launched Windows Hello[13] for supported devices, bringing face-recognition to modern laptops.

2017: Four years after Apple brought the fingerprint to the masses, they launched FaceID, an embedded[14] array of sensors with the iPhone X, to perform face-based authentication used to unlock devices, approve payments, and other critical actions.

Biometrics in Our Lives Today

Think about it In less than ten seconds, can you name three ways your biometric data is being used every day?

Having discussed an example of emerging issues of biometric data in specialized areas, in this section we set out to provide an overview of how biometrics are being used in day-to-day life. We will discuss the ways technological advances have made biometrics accessible to vastly more people since the start of the 21st century. In later chapters, we will dive more deeply into the implications of this growth.

---

[11] https://abcnews.go.com/Technology/story?id=98871&page=1#:~:text=Facefinder%20picked%20out%2019%20people,police%20spokesman%20Joe%20Durkin%20said.

[12] Fingerprint in iPhone 5s 2013 www.howtogeek.com/802122/which-iphones-have-touch-id/.

[13] https://blogs.windows.com/windowsexperience/2015/07/25/say-hello-to-windows-hello-on-windows-10/

[14] FaceID https://apple.fandom.com/wiki/Face_ID.

CHAPTER 1   THE GROWING USE OF BIOMETRICS

Where We Encounter Biometrics

There are many situations where the things we do and the tools we use take advantage of some sort of biometric signal our body provides.

- Personal Devices/Home:
    - Smartphones
    - Smartwatches/Fitness trackers
    - Home assistants/Smart speakers
    - Laptop/Tablets/Computers
    - Home security systems
    - Smart doorbells
    - Smart TVs
- Public Spaces:
    - Train stations
    - Airports
    - Hospitals
    - Shopping Malls
    - Biometric passports for travel and identification

The way we interact with these devices and applications can vary significantly. While unlocking a smartphone using a fingerprint or speaking to our smart speaker to find out the weather forecast requires conscious action, other situations in which our human characteristics are used do not require us to take action—and may even happen without us being aware.

CHAPTER 1   THE GROWING USE OF BIOMETRICS

Cameras in Public Spaces

The number of cameras deployed in public spaces has grown in recent years. In the UK alone, it is estimated that a total of 7.3 million cameras[15] have been installed in public spaces. A typical UK resident may have their image captured up to 70 times per day. One estimate is that a Londoner can expect to be captured on CCTV up to 300 times per day.

The UK is not alone in relying on CCTV to maintain order. More and more, this is becoming a selected method of monitoring public spaces. Table 1-1 shows camera usage in various countries.

Table 1-1. Estimated CCTV cameras in public spaces[16]

Country	CCTV cameras deployed (estimate)
China	200 million
USA	50 million
UK	7–8 million
Germany	~5 million
Japan	~5 million
Vietnam	2.6 million
France	1.6 million

Cities tend to have higher density of surveillance cameras; the following table provides interesting insights into the most surveilled cities[17] in the world.

---

[15] 2022 cameras per country https://clarionuk.com/resources/how-many-cctv-cameras-are-in-london/#:~:text=in%20the%20UK%3F-,R.

[16] CCT per country https://upcomingsecurity.co.uk/security-guides/cctv-camera-guides/cctv-by-country/ www.comparitech.com/vpn-privacy/the-worlds-most-surveilled-cities/.

[17] Most surveilled cities www.comparitech.com/vpn-privacy/the-worlds-most-surveilled-cities/.

CHAPTER 1   THE GROWING USE OF BIOMETRICS

City/cities	Cameras per 1,000 people
China (data only available for the country)	439
Hyderabad, India	83
Indore, India	60
Delhi, India	20
Singapore, Singapore	18
Moscow, Russia	16.8
Baghdad, Iraq	15.5
Seoul, South Korea	14.5
St. Petersburg, Russia	13.5
London, England (UK)	13.2

Purpose of Cameras in Public Spaces

Most cameras are likely to keep recorded data for a defined period of time in case law enforcement or the operators of the camera need to look at the footage. We wouldn't call this a use of biometric traits per se, since no specific features are extracted from the video footage. We will cover feature extraction in a later chapter.

A fairly common use of cameras in public spaces is crowd control. In this case, the system analyzes the number of people present at each time. Detecting the presence of human life is a use of biometric information.

13

CHAPTER 1   THE GROWING USE OF BIOMETRICS

Personal Devices

According to studies conducted, the average person looks at their smartphone 150 times a day.[18] If you use a more modern device, chances are that every time you look at your phone, it kind of looks back at you. With the launch of iPhoneX in 2017, Apple replaced a fingerprint sensor used to unlock iPhones with a complex camera system called FaceID. Other vendors have since implemented a variety of similar systems. It is estimated that by 2024, 1.3 billion personal devices will be able to conduct some level of facial recognition. This steep development is meaningful as it allows developers and regulators to adopt new methods and requirements based on the broad availability of these features.

Biometrics are also increasingly used on laptops. Many of the middle and upper tier laptops now offer a fingerprint option for machine login. This means that instead of typing a password or code to access the machine, a user can provide their fingerprint. Another widely available option for machine login is Windows Hello, a Microsoft proprietary feature that allows the users to unlock their computer using the built-in webcam to perform facial recognition checks.

A category of personal devices that has come up in the last decade using various types of biometric signals from the start are smartwatches. Worn on the wrist, they use light-based sensors to detect and measure heart rate, blood pressure, and other related human characteristics. Beyond smartwatches, there are many similar wearable devices like fitness trackers and smart rings. These devices take similar types of measurements of biometric signals on the wrist or finger of the user, and analyze hand orientation and movement to create motion patterns.

---

[18] www.inc.com/john-brandon/these-updated-stats-about-how-often-we-use-our-phones-will-humble-you.html accessed 29 April 2023.

The popularity of these wearable devices is skyrocketing. The global market is expected to grow from $61 billion in 2022 to more than $110 billion as soon as 2028.[19]

Biometrics at Home

The following sections highlight common forms of biometrics many people encounter in their homes on a daily basis.

Video-Enabled Doorbells

Devices that use our human characteristics to function, beyond just the smartphone and personal computer, have become ubiquitous. As mentioned at the start of this chapter, 16% of US households have installed a Video-Enabled doorbell and forecasters expect 17% year-of-year growth[20] in this number. We literally use biometrics at our doorsteps. These devices are capable of detecting faces and, in many cases, comparing them to a set of known faces.

Most of the needs supported by these video-enabled doorbells can be summed up as personalization. The images collected by the camera can be used on multiple levels:

1. **Notice activity**: Is there movement of any sort in the field of view of the video-enabled doorbell?

2. **Categorize activity**: Being able to differentiate between various sources of movement. Is it a human, animal, car, or something else?

---

[19] Global wearable market www.grandviewresearch.com/industry-analysis/wearable-technology-market#:~:text=Report%20Overview,14.6%25%20from%202023%20to%202030.

[20] www.consumerreports.org/home-garden/home-security-cameras/best-video-doorbells-of-the-year-a111542607.

3. **Identify the person**: Is this person a member of the household, a recurring guest, or a stranger?

4. **Hear**: Smart doorbells generally also have the ability to capture or record audio. Said audio signal can be used for similar purposes as the video feed.

Many video doorbells allow their owners to make decisions based upon the answers to these questions. These decisions can be limited to the type of notification they want to receive or if the system should record and keep the video-images for further inspection.

In regard to transparency of the use of collected data, it's comparable to the situation described regarding CCTV. The person delivering your pizza won't know if their image is being stored, compared to the faces of your family members, or possibly even used to find a fugitive last seen in your neighborhood. While the General Data Protection Regulation (GDPR) also regulates the collection of data by individuals, the issue here is more practical in nature than legal. In this book, we won't dive into the details of how GDPR applies in this case and won't mention related cases in which this topic has been handled. We want you to be aware of the practical issues cameras pointing away from private properties can cause. Since this is not a publication covering the legal aspects, we're keeping this part light.

In some areas, these video-doorbells have reached a level of market penetration that law enforcement are making use of recordings. Frequently, information regarding a crime can be gleaned from doorbell recordings. Police departments at an increasing rate are petitioning homeowners and vendors for access to these stored videos.

Smart Devices

Since the launch of the Amazon Alexa Smart Speaker in 2014, other manufacturers like Google and Apple have followed suit. Nearly ten years later, there are approximately 95 million smart speakers installed in the United States.

CHAPTER 1   THE GROWING USE OF BIOMETRICS

Another type of device that has received the "Smart" prefix in recent years is the television. In order to deliver more personalized experiences and content-suggestions, some vendors have started using built-in cameras to identify who is sitting in front of the TV. The ability to detect and recognize the audience faces and match them to a household member allows a traditionally shared device to offer more personalized content and settings.

How Biometrics Became So Ubiquitous

What has driven this rapid growth? It's clear there is a market for the convenience and added security we can gain by utilizing biometric signals, but why now? What has been the tipping point allowing the use of biometric data to explode? Looking back at the first decades of the 21st century there are a few driving factors that have supported this steep adoption curve:

- Cheaper and smaller sensors
- Increased computing power
- Greater connectivity

It Starts with the Sensors

A huge factor in the rapid expansion of the use of biometrics is the falling cost of producing and implementing sensors that allow device manufacturers to integrate them into their hardware solutions.

Fingerprint sensors, as used in smartphones, tablets, laptops, and other devices have significantly gone down in costs over the past years. While the average price of such a sensor was around $5.50 in 2014, it has come down to $2 in 2020.[21]

---

[21] www.bayometric.com/biometric-devices-cost/.

Sensors, which measure and analyze biometric data have not only become cheaper but smaller as well. This allows them to be integrated into more devices. Between 2014 and 2018, the worldwide share of smartphones shipped with fingerprint sensors[22] rose from 19% (2014) to 60% (2018).

Devices with facial recognition capabilities reached 64% in 2022 compared to just 5% in 2017. As these numbers grow, application developers can rely on the availability of these features and increasingly depend on them. While just a few years ago, only a small percent of the population was able to benefit from these technologies, they have fast become commonplace.

Processing Power Is More Readily Available

Data collected by sensors must be processed to be useful. The required processing power becomes more readily available as the devices we use—smartphones, computers, wearables—are built with more powerful processors. The capacity to perform centralized processing—a.k.a. in the cloud—is increasing and becoming cheaper.

We have never had as much capacity in our hands and in figurative arm's reach as we do today. There's no reason to doubt that this statement will be true no matter when you read this book.

Bandwidth and Connectivity

We truly live in the age of connectivity. There are fewer and fewer situations where we can't transfer large amounts of data from our local devices to the powerful centralized computers called "the cloud" that perform complex computations to analyze the biometrics and provide the expected output.

---

[22] www.insiderintelligence.com/content/how-do-consumers-feel-about-biometrics.

Research funded by the European Union states that in 2021 97% of all households in Europe had access to a fixed or cellular broadband access network offering at least 2 Mbps of download speed.[23] This type of broadband access is sufficient for people to access digital services offered by financial institutions or governments that often require authentication based on biometrics to access their services. More recent iterations of the cellular data standards (e.g., 4G or 5G) and other Wireless transport options are also more optimized to accommodate the needs of large numbers of sensors like cameras to collect biometric data.

Summary

The rate at which technology detects and analyzes our human characteristics has skyrocketed in the first decades of the 21st century. In contrast to the previous decades during which biometric technology was only accessible for specialized use, this evolution represents a profound shift in who has access to these capabilities—and who is exposed to them.

The implications of this rapid change are numerous and varied. Personalization can make many aspects of our lives easier and increased security can reduce the risk of fraud and harm. It is also important to recognize that there are also risks and trade-offs that come with these changes. As a society and as individuals, we need to understand these risks in order to make informed trade-off decisions regarding the technology we embrace. As this book progresses, we will develop a deeper understanding of these risks and consider them from various angles.

In the next chapter, we will solidify our understanding of the basics around biometric data—what it is, what it does, and how it is used.

---

[23] https://digital-strategy.ec.europa.eu/en/library/broadband-coverage-europe-2021.

CHAPTER 2

What Are Biometrics?

Now that we've had a look at how the field of biometrics has evolved and how its use has spread in the last decades, let's firm up some underpinning ideas. In this chapter, we'll lay the groundwork of what biometric data is, what it is used for, and very generally how it is used.

What Is Biometric Data?

The term *biometrics* is commonly used to mean the **signals** that can indicate the presence, state, and identity of living beings based on physiological or behavioral features.

With *bio-* coming from the Greek for *life* and *-metric* having roots in several languages and meaning *of or about measurement*, *biometric* can be defined as *pertaining to measurement of a living thing*.

In this book, we also use the terms *biometrics* and *biometric data*. While we don't make a significant distinction between the terms, essentially we will consider the terms as follows:

> *Biometric: Measurement of physical, physiological, or behavioral characteristics*

> *Biometric Data: Raw information gathered by a sensor*

CHAPTER 2   WHAT ARE BIOMETRICS?

Some sources of biometric data are fingerprints, heart rate, voice, walking patterns, and even typing patterns. As you can imagine from this wide range of examples, not all types of biometric data support the same use case or provide equal value.

Traits and Features

When exploring the realm of biometrics, it is essential to distinguish between the terms "Traits" and "Features."

Traits refer to the specific types of biometric identifiers that can be measured. Common examples include fingerprints, voice, facial recognition, and heart rate. Each trait is unique in how it can be captured and the type of information it provides about an individual.

Within each biometric trait, there are multiple distinct characteristics, or features, that can be extracted and analyzed. These features provide the detailed data necessary for identifying or verifying the identity of an individual or assessing their liveness or health. See Table 2-1 for examples of features and how they might be used.

Table 2-1. Traits and corresponding features

Trait	Features	Purpose/use
Face	Head posture, eye status (open/closed)	Used in security systems and user authentication
Voice	Volume, speed, pauses	Helpful in speaker verification and sentiment analysis
Heart Rate	Beat irregularity, rhythm	Used in health monitoring for detecting arrhythmias
Fingerprint	Ridge ending, bifurcation	Commonly used in forensic analysis and access control

What Is Biometric Data Used For?

As we pointed out in Chapter 1, biometric data is being used more and more frequently in more and more contexts. But, the question here is different. What purpose does it serve? When a product is created that makes use of biometric data, what is the motivation behind its use? Applications of biometric data are used to solve problems.

Types of Problems Solved Using Biometrics

If we look at some of the examples where biometrics are used, and play a visible role in solving problems, we can divide these problems into three categories:

Who are you?	Match someone's biometric traits to existing records in order to verify their identity.
How are you?	Use the vital signs to assess the state of this being.
Are you real?	Determine if a real living being is present.

Who Are You?

This is likely the one we're most aware of encountering in our daily lives. Whenever we use biometric traits like a fingerprint or our faces to unlock our smartphones, perform a payment with a system like Apple Pay, or ask our home assistant for our schedule for the day—that's when the problem of identifying "who we are" is being assessed.

In this case, one or multiple types of biometrics are being detected and compared to one or multiple models that were previously collected. If one of them matches with a reasonable level of confidence, a match takes place.

CHAPTER 2   WHAT ARE BIOMETRICS?

A more precise way to describe the way we use our biometrics to access personalized services could be "Are you who you pretend to be?" In this case, the person wanting to be identified provides some type of identifier that acts as a declaration of who they are. In many cases, this can be a username, email address, phone number, or account number. Although this piece of information is not necessarily secret, it allows the system to compare the person's identity with a defined model and isolate it from other models (see Table 2-2).

One use of biometric information, centered around the face, which we're going to mention in this book is the process of "selfie-matching." A selfie-match is the process of assessing if the person in front of the camera is the person depicted on a government issued document like a passport. Historically, this was done by a trained professional like an immigration officer, bank teller, etc. that would compare a document with the face of the person in front of them. The term selfie-match was coined in recent years, when many of these identity verification steps moved online. You might have created a bank account recently online and encountered a process where you had to upload a picture of a driver's license or passport and then take a selfie of yourself using the front-facing camera of your device. In the background, the service provider then would run a facial recognition algorithm and assess the likelihood of the face on the document being from the same person as the one captured in real time.

Think about it   Have you done a selfie-match? What traits and features do you think are being assessed to determine if your face watches the provided document?

Table 2-2. *Context of identity match*

Scope	Objective	Examples
One to one	Compare the biometrics detected from one person with the one model that is stored for the context.	Comparison of someone's face to a government issued ID Fingerprint detection to access laptop
One to many	Compare the biometrics detected from one person with multiple models stored for the context.	Voice Identification of family or household members for Voice-Activated speakers A space where multiple people have access.
Many to one	Compare the biometrics detected from multiple people with one model stored for the context.	CCTV cameras searching for a specific individual (e.g., criminals)

One to One Matching

When we unlock our smartphones or use biometrics to login to an online account, the system is comparing a biometric trait with a model that has been previously recorded. The sample and reference are being compared and a probability for them being the same is being assessed by the algorithm. The algorithm then provides a confidence score, usually between 0 and 1, where 1 is absolute confidence, based on which the system decides to consider the sample as correct or not.

The vast majority of authentication systems that use biometrics are based on the principle that the person trying to authenticate first provides a piece of information on who they pretend to be. This can be an email address, username, account number, or some sort of digital signature. If the identifier provided exists on the system, they may be prompted to authenticate using a biometric trait like a fingerprint, voice command, etc.

This means that the system only compares the provided biometric signal to the one associated with said identifier. Even if the biometric trait exists linked to another identifier, this would not allow the person to authenticate into either of the accounts.

One to Many

Another way biometric signals are often used—while less prominently experienced by consumers—is matching a biometric trait with a dataset to identify if a match with high confidence is present. In these cases, the system looks for the sample(s) with the highest confidence score.

The size of the dataset changes the requirements on how accurately the trait must be collected in order for a reliable assessment to be made.

The first nursery our daughter visited had a fingerprint scanner to open the front door. Parents could either ring the buzzer and wait for staff to let them in—and be prepared to show evidence of identity—or enroll their fingerprint under supervision of an employee of the nursery and use it to access the building in the future. The dataset of fingerprints in this case unlikely exceeded a few hundred fingerprints.

Many to One

Biometric signals being used in a Many to 1 context are much less common and possibly even unknown to the target person. An example of this would be any situation in which many sample signals are checked to determine if they match a specific template. The case given in the chart references searching CCTV footage to find a specific person of interest.

How Are You?

Many of our vital signs can provide information about how well our body is performing. In our daily lives, we encounter them in applications meant to help us become more active, achieve movement goals, and track our activity, using biometric information like pulse, heart rate, blood oxidation levels as a way of record keeping.

Personal Record Keeping

Fitness and activity trackers come in a variety of form factors. They can be single-purpose devices, part of a wearable with broader capabilities, or purely in the form of software running on a smartphone (see Table 2-3).

Table 2-3. Form factors for vital sign collection

Form factor	Examples of products
Single-purpose devices—made for a specific use	Fitness trackers from companies like Fitbit, Garmin, Polar
Wearables with broader capabilities	Smartwatches like Apple Watch, Samsung Galaxy Watch, Smart rings, Smart glasses
Fitness applications on smartphones	Fitness and tracking applications like Apple Health, Nike training, Strava, etc.

CHAPTER 2   WHAT ARE BIOMETRICS?

These devices or applications collect data like our step-count and heart rate to assess our overall level of activity during the day or at specific times—when we tell them that we're doing some exercise, for one. Having the ability to collect this data gives these applications the ability to provide us with trends in our levels of activity:

- Are we reaching our goals?
- Is our level of activity trending up or down?
- How do we compare with others in our friend or age-group?

Medical Analysis

Using biometric signals is also used to perform short- and long-term health assessments. Measurements like height, weight, and blood pressure are part of most medical check-ups and help medical professionals understand the current and long-term development of our health.

Genetic markers are a type of biometric information that can be used to make medical assessments.

The use of physiological and behavioral biometric traits can be useful ways to understand short-term conditions or longer term developments.

The type of biometric analysis made for medical purpose can be broadly be divided into three categories:

1) Vital Signs: Measurement of traits like heart rate, blood pressure, etc.

2) Imaging: Creating images of externally invisible characteristics like MRI, X-Scan, etc.

3) Biochemical Markers: Analysis of the blood for specific substances

Sentiment Analysis

When we communicate with each other, we constantly observe each other's mood. This can be done based on the choice of words, tone of voice, facial expressions, and body posture. If some of these signals aren't available to us, we tend to focus on what we have, reducing the accuracy of our interpretation of the other person's state of mind, mood, and sentiments.

There are significant research efforts going on to use technology to assess someone's sentiments when communicating.

The use of behavioral biometrics such as voice, gait, typing patterns, etc. can be an indication of sentiment as they can directly be impacted by the person's mood and mental state.

Are You Real?

When using biometric signals to draw conclusions that, if wrong, could have a significantly negative impact either of monetary or other type, it is important to have confidence in the integrity of the signal. One of these approaches is called liveness. Many of our biometric traits like voice, face, and even fingerprints can be stolen by someone with bad intentions. In these cases, we want to use additional signals that make us more confident that we're dealing with a real person.

In some cases, like at the immigration desk at the airport, this task can (partially) be given to a human. Whenever the biometric integrity is assessed through a process without human supervision, this has to be covered by technology. Liveness can be assessed by using one or multiple other biometric traits at the time of collecting the primary trait.

Being able to assess proof of live human presence makes the conclusions drawn based on the biometric signals more reliable. Especially in situations where regulatory requirements mandate that the service provider (e.g., banks) authenticate their customers with a high level of confidence, assessing liveness can be as important as matching the biometric factors with a high level of confidence.

Most modern biometric systems have some element of liveness check embedded in order to detect spoofed biometric information like a silicone fingerprint, pre-recorded voice, or a printed face.

Dorothy E. Denning, also called "the Godmother of liveness" once said that "It's 'liveness', not secrecy, that counts."[1] Due to the increasing importance and use of liveness checks, we dedicated a separate chapter to this subject.

Identifying the Problem Being Addressed

A helpful approach to understanding the opportunities of new or newly available technology is to first clearly identify the problem that needs to be addressed and then understand the limitations and external requirements.

Although some biometrics are great for one type of problem in one situation, they might not be suitable for a different set of circumstances.

When assessing which problems can be solved with the use of biometrics, it is important to reflect on the type of conclusion that is being drawn based on the biometric information and what the implications are of getting it wrong. In Chapter 6, we address more about accuracy, precision, and false negatives/false positives. Chapter 8 will provide a critical analysis of some drawbacks and limitations inherent in the use of biometrics.

Reading and assessing a biometric signal depends on a lot of factors for accuracy, and even in best cases there is always a chance of an error. The conclusion that is being drawn based on the biometric signals must be clearly defined well in advance.

---

[1] Dorothy E. Denings liveness not secrecy www.liveness.com/.

The Journey of Biometric Data

In this section, we'll look into the journey a biometric signal takes from beginning to end of an individual process. To arrive at the desired outcome of answering one of the three major questions—*Who are you? How are you?* and *Are you real?*—there are four high-level steps of what must happen.

Acquiring a biometric signal is only one part of the journey that should lead to a desired outcome. In order to understand the opportunities and challenges, we need to split the journey into the following high-level steps:

1. Signal acquisition—gathering raw data
2. Signal processing/feature extraction
3. Data storage
4. Comparison and Matching
5. Decision-making
6. Action
7. Adaption (learning ability)

Signal Acquisition (Collection)

The biometric journey starts with having the ability to identify and acquire a signal that represents a human characteristic. These characteristics can vary in how **unique** they are to a specific person, how **consistent** they are for a given person over time, and how **reliably** they can be measured.

To identify a biometric signal, some type of sensor needs to be used. Some biometric signals require specific, single-purpose sensors to be identified and collected and others can be collected with more methods. In this context, we consider a sensor to be a piece of hardware that can identify and collect one or more human characteristics and translate it into a digital signal that can be measured and processed.

One example can be voice-detection and recognition. The sensor in use here is a microphone that listens for input of audio-waves within the expected frequency of human voice (80–180Hz for adult men and 165–255 Hz for adult women).[2] With the human voice, it's likely that additional noise from the surroundings is coming in. In order to make the desired signal usable for biometric use cases, said noise needs to be filtered out.

Sensors might use the visible light spectrum, electromagnetic fields, infrared, or sound waves.

Signal Processing and Feature Extraction

Taking this signal and translating it into a form that can be transferred, stored, and processed is the next step. Imagine the input being a noisy, sometimes fragmented, analog signal that then needs to be cleaned and translated into numbers and data. Depending on the features that need to be processed based on the specific trait(s), they have to be extracted using dedicated algorithms.

Coming back to the voice example, the audio signal needs to be translated into a voice model to compare it to a reference if used for identification. The recorded (and cleaned) voice signal has to be translated into a voice model that then can be compared to a previously created model using the same algorithm.

Once the data has been processed, some provision must be made for the **storage** of this data. Consideration must be given regarding the length of time the data should be stored and where it will be stored.

---

[2] Frequency of human voice `https://flypaper.soundfly.com/produce/eqing-vocals-whats-happening-in-each-frequency-range-in-the-human-voice/#:~:text=The%20Frequencies%20We%20Can%20Hear&text=During%20a%20conversation%2C%20the%20fundamental,the%20%E2%80%9Cspeech%20frequency%20band.%E2%80%9D`

Data Storage

When a company first takes a special kind of personal measurement like your fingerprint or voice for identification, they transform it into a code that represents you, also called embeddings. This code, which doesn't show your actual fingerprint or face, is what the company saves in their system. Just like any personal detail, this information needs to be kept safe.

Companies are required to protect it by making sure only the right people can see it and that the information doesn't change or get damaged. They often use a digital lock, known as encryption, to keep this data secure. If someone were to try to steal this data, the digital lock would prevent them from understanding it. Moreover, laws in many places, like in Europe and parts of the United States, are strict about ensuring your personal information are kept private and used only for identifying who you are or confirming it's really you.

Comparison and Matching

Matching biometric signals to templates—previously stored models that represent the instances of a biometric trait—typically involves pattern recognition technologies that can work in a few different ways, depending on the type of biometric data and the specific application. Here are some of the common methods:

> **Minutiae Matching for Fingerprints**: The most common method for fingerprint matching is minutiae matching. Minutiae points are specific points on a fingerprint, like where ridges end or split. The matching algorithm compares the minutiae points of a newly captured fingerprint with those in the stored templates.

Pattern Matching: Pattern matching involves comparing the overall pattern of the biometric trait, such as the visual pattern of an iris or the geometric pattern of a face, against stored templates.

Feature Matching: This involves extracting specific features from the biometric sample, like the relative positions of facial features (eyes, nose, mouth), and then comparing these features to those in the stored template.

Template Matching: Template matching directly compares the value of the biometric sample against the templates. This could be comparing the entire raw biometric data set against the template, which is often computationally intensive.

Statistical/Probabilistic Matching: This method relies on the probability of matches based on statistical analysis. It often involves more complex algorithms that can handle variations or noise in the biometric data.

Neural Networks and Deep Learning: Machine learning, particularly deep learning methods, can be employed for biometric matching. Neural networks can learn to recognize complex patterns within biometric data and can be very effective, especially in facial recognition.

The exact method used can vary widely based on the application, the desired level of security, and the acceptable trade-off between false positives and false negatives. Regardless of the method, the goal is to accurately determine whether the biometric sample matches the stored template, taking into account the potential for variations in the samples.

Decision-Making

Whether a biometric signal is being matched with a template or a series of signals are being used to come to a conclusion of integrity, health, sentiment, activity, etc. decisions based on biometric information is in nature probabilistic.

There are a few common ways that decisions based on physiological or behavioral biometric signals are taken:

- Threshold setting: The decision is based on defined thresholds regarding the biometric information.

- Fixed FAR or FRR: By using a fixed False Acceptance Rate or False Rejection Rate, an accurate matching can be defined.

- Machine learning and AI are increasingly leading to improved decision-making of biometric systems. These models can learn from larger datasets.

Action

Although the result may be in the form of a yes or no, or perhaps a confidence score, the system utilizing the process will initiate an action based on the result. This action could be granting access to an account or device, or generating a warning to indicate that a heart rate is at a dangerous level.

Adaption

Increasing use of machine learning and artificial intelligence systems utilizing biometrics allow the constant adaptation of algorithms or even templates to improve the decision-making, performance, and robustness against adversarial attacks like spoofing.

CHAPTER 2 WHAT ARE BIOMETRICS?

Summary

Chapter 2 explores the fundamental aspects of biometrics, shedding an initial light on what biometric data encompasses and its diverse applications across various fields. We began by defining some essential terms. Then we addressed the question of what biometric data is used for. Biometric data is used to answer the questions Who are you? How are you? Are you real? We followed biometric data through its journey from signal acquisition through to adaption.

In chapter 3, we round out Part 1 by considering adversarial behavior, its role in the development of the field of biometrics, and how biometric systems are designed to thwart attacks.

CHAPTER 3

Adversarial Behavior—Attack and Defense

Now that we've built a firm understanding of what biometric data can be used for, Chapter 3 discusses how we try to ensure success—by addressing adversarial behavior. This chapter provides a preliminary description of types of attack, factors that go into implementing an attack, and approaches to defending biometric systems.

Attacks—Bad Actions

One of the most common purposes of using biometrics is to increase the cost of bad actions. Such bad actions can range from attempting fraudulent access to someone's digital information, impersonating someone in order to appear as them, or generally feeding false biometric information into a system that then comes to the wrong conclusions.

CHAPTER 3   ADVERSARIAL BEHAVIOR—ATTACK AND DEFENSE

Make Bad Actions More Expensive

When we think about these fraudsters, hackers, scammers, cyber criminals, etc. as people motivated to perform some type of bad actions, the use of biometrics is often meant to lower their success rate and make their operation more expensive. If gaining unauthorized access to an email account takes 10 minutes or 10 hours, it is a significant difference in how much they can achieve with their available resources. Making these efforts more expensive is also making them less economically viable for the cyber criminals.

Time—Expertise—Equipment

One approach to make this concept more tangible can be to assess the cost to perform a bad action is by splitting up the sophistication of attacks using the factors of time, expertise, and equipment

- Time: How long does it take an attacker to trick a protection mechanism?

- Expertise: How much expertise does this require? Can it be done by a single layperson or does it need a group of experts with various types of skills

- Equipment: What equipment is needed? Can a simple printer do the job or does it need expensive, rare, and specialized equipment?

Understanding this mental model of making badness more expensive and assessing the cost to bypass a specific protection is a useful skill when thinking about the effectiveness of biometrics. If you understand that nothing is 100% secure, but understand the effort someone might reasonably put into it, the adequate level of protection can be identified.

In order to demonstrate their ability to detect spoofed biometric material trying to bypass their facial recognition technology, FaceTec has launched a bounty program[1] in which it encourages security researchers to show proof of their ability to bypass their liveness checks. If successful, the researcher is financially compensated. FaceTec reports that more than 130,000 spoofing attempts have been submitted during the first 40 months since launching the program.

General Types of Attacks

When it comes down to biometrics, the types of attacks or, more generally speaking, bad actions, can be split into the following categories:

- **Spoofing**: Using fake biometric data, like a photograph or a 3D mask, to trick a biometric system into thinking it's the real person.

- **Replay Attacks**: Reusing previously captured biometric data, such as a recorded voice or a video, to gain unauthorized access.

- **Synthetic Biometrics**: Creating artificial biometric data, such as computer-generated fingerprints or faces, to fool a biometric system.

- **Phishing**: Deceiving individuals into providing their biometric data through fake websites or communication channels.

- **Brute Force Attacks**: Systematically trying many different biometric inputs until finding one that works to gain unauthorized access.

---

[1] FaceTec Bounty Program https://dev.facetec.com/spoof-bounty-program.

- **Tampering**: Manipulating the biometric sensor or data to alter or bypass the verification process.

- **Template Inversion**: Reconstructing the original biometric trait from stored biometric templates to create a fake biometric input.

- **Mimicry**: Imitating someone's biometric traits, like their voice or mannerisms, to deceive a biometric system.

Artificial Intelligence (AI) to Attack Biometrics

Talking about biometrics without addressing the significant impact of Artificial Intelligence (AI) would be a missed opportunity. While this book is not meant to be a comprehensive resource on AI and Machine Learning (ML), it's important to have a basic understanding of how these technologies relate to biometrics.

In recent years, both the awareness of AI and the availability of tools to use it have skyrocketed. Many people have heard of or even used tools like ChatGPT to generate text and images based on text input. This is an example of Generative AI—AI used to create desired outputs.

Using Generative AI to bypass or provide false information to a biometric system involves creating outputs like an image of a face or a spoofed recording of someone's voice, intending to trick the system into accepting it as authentic biometric information. The use of AI-generated artifacts for malicious purposes can significantly reduce the cost of conducting sophisticated attacks on biometric systems. Generative AI has made it cheaper and easier to spoof real people's biometric traits with higher quality and on a larger scale. However, it's important to understand that these attacks, while more accessible, are still expensive and often not economically viable for targeting certain individuals or organizations.

CHAPTER 3   ADVERSARIAL BEHAVIOR—ATTACK AND DEFENSE

Examples of Attacks Against Biometrics

Attack against systems that use biometric signals are not just theoretical in nature. With increased use of said technologies to protect a broad variety of systems, infrastructure, and potentially valuable information, the adversarial ecosystem has increased in maturity.

While stealing biometric information—either from the source (meaning the people) or databases that store traits like fingerprints, picture faces, voice models, etc.—has and will continue to occur, it's not always the most cost-effective method for the attacker to pursue their fraudulent activities.

Stolen Biometric Data

One way biometric information can be used to perform attacks against individuals is to obtain previously collected biometric information. During a cyber-incident in 2015 against the US Office of Personnel Management (OPM),[2] an estimated 5.6 Million fingerprints were obtained by the attackers. If said set of fingerprints also contained information on who they belonged to, this could be a valuable dataset for attackers who want to perform attacks against individuals whose biometric data was included in the hack.

The actual usefulness of this information to access bank accounts, unlock smartphones, enter highly secured buildings, etc. then would require the bad actors to turn the digitally saved representations of the stolen biometrics into a physical model to trick the targeted systems.

The bigger risk of attacks like these is considered to be the ability to connect fingerprints to real-world identities across multiple systems.

---

[2] 2015 hack against OPM www.washingtonpost.com/news/the-switch/wp/2015/09/23/opm-now-says-more-than-five-million-fingerprints-compromised-in-breaches/.

Artificially Created Information

Another type of attack can include the use of "publicly" available information like pictures, video, or audio recordings to create artifacts with biometric traits to spoof a system. With the use of Artificial Intelligence (AI) algorithms, artifacts like spoken language or even videos containing moving images and sound can be made with a varied degree of quality.

Said artifacts can then be used on systems that use audio or video input to verify an individual.

Potential Future Threats

With improvements in the area of generative artificial intelligence algorithms and cheaper computational resources, the (re)creation of biometric information for malicious purposes will be cheaper and more widely available.

The big trend in technology from the 2020s is without a doubt the rise of Artificial Intelligence which boosted the ability to create digital information at reduced cost. While the use of AI to break into buildings, systems, bank accounts, etc. has been a subject for security researchers, real-world attacks are not yet as common as the media reports of recent years imply. As older protection systems such as passwords are losing relevance, attacks against the biometric system will become the more economically viable avenue for attackers. It's safe to predict that the use of generative AI will play a big role in this.

Generative AI alone in combination with broader availability of training data poses a growing risk of systems that use biometric information for identification or authentication reasons.

Defense

On the other side of the attack, there's the need and ability to defend, in order to make these bad actions more expensive. While the use of biometrics itself can be seen as a defense mechanism to make attacks against digital identities more expensive, there are also ways to use more biometric signals to defend against said bad action.

Layered Approach

In most cases, where biometrics are used to prevent unauthorized access, the authorization happens by layering multiple factors on top of each other. Generally speaking, this can be split into the following types of factors that are being combined with biometrics:

- Knowledge factor—Something you know: This can be a password, a phrase, etc. that ideally only the authorized person knows

- Possession factor—Something you have: A physical key, debit/credit card, smartphone, etc. can act as a possession factor. In these cases, the biometric factor can only be used on previously vetted possession factors. One-time codes delivered via SMS or other channels can also be seen as possession factors.

Liveness

At this point, it makes sense to discuss the concept of Liveness in a general approach. While not the only defense against attack against biometrics, it's a very fundamental one.

CHAPTER 3   ADVERSARIAL BEHAVIOR—ATTACK AND DEFENSE

A good biometric system should not depend on secrecy
...biometric prints cannot be kept secret, but the validation process must check for liveness of the readings *(Dorothy E. Denning)*

Liveness is the ability of assessing if a biometric signal actually comes from a living human at the time and place of collection. Dorothy E. Denning, also known as "the Godmother of liveness," coined the quote that started this chapter. Similarly to the Turing-Tests efforts to assess the presence of "human-like-abilities," a liveness-check is built to assess the presence of a human being when and where a biometric signal is extracted.

This table describes what type of fraudulent input a liveness test is looking for:

Fraudulent input type	Description
Spoof	Artificially created signals based on collected biometric information from a specific real person
Replay	1:1 replay of a previously collected biometric trait from a specific person
Synthetically generated biometrics	Biometric information generated from a fictional person that doesn't exist

Denning's statement underlines the fact that we can't assume that our biometric traits can be held secret, but how we can increase trust in them when they're being used.

When we look at the most common biometric traits, they either "stay behind" like your fingerprints, "travel" like your voice, or can be captured (with a good camera) when it's your face, iris, retina, gait, etc. This doesn't mean that biometrics don't work or that they are as bad as passwords when it comes to protecting your personal information. It just means that the integrity of a signal pretending to provide biometric information needs to be analyzed to be from a live person. One or multiple liveness checks have to be made in order to assess if the system is being used by a real human or the biometric signal has been spoofed (faked), injected (replayed from its original source), or artificially created.

The Utopia to Keep Biometrics Secret

It is unrealistic to keep our biometric traits to ourselves. Just think about how many places your biometrics have been "left behind" today. All the surfaces you touched with your fingertips, all the cameras from CCTV, smartphones, video-enabled doorbells, etc. that have "seen" your face or captured you walking by, and all the times your voice could've been recorded.

We rarely have full control over where our biometric information is left. Fingerprints, for example, are per definition left on any surface we touch, much to the frustration of criminals. Our voice travels across rooms, and digital channels, allowing others to hear and potentially record it. Many other biometric traits can be captured—some with more effort than others, but none of them can fully be kept a secret.

If we google our names, many of us will likely find one or multiple images of ourselves on the Internet. Said 2D images contain biometric information. But we shouldn't assume that any biometric check that uses our face is now useless because other people have access to one or multiple images of our face. This is where liveness comes into play. Devices like modern iPhones (iPhone X and newer), which in addition to capturing a 2D image by using the front facing camera can also directly acquire 3D features of the face while using additional infrared sensors, have the ability to perform liveness and biometric checks that can't be spoofed with a 2D image alone printed on paper. Most face verification algorithms have to rely on a series of 2D images due to the lack of

CHAPTER 3   ADVERSARIAL BEHAVIOR—ATTACK AND DEFENSE

dedicated hardware as described earlier. When using image data that are based on the two dimensions, liveness methods can infer 3D biometric information from a 2D+time sequence of images.

Specialized hardware, used in the example of modern iPhones, lead to increased accuracy due to the depth information that can be collected to assess the actual dimensions and depth of a face.

Goal to Check for Liveness

The goal of performing a liveness check is to assess, with high enough confidence, that the biometric feature has been extracted from a real (live) person and hasn't been reproduced by software or replayed by the attacker.

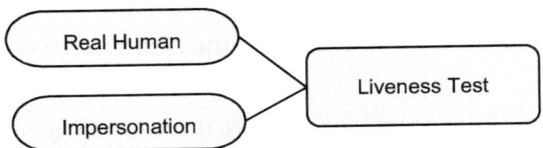

When processing a biometric trait, a liveness check can either use some of the extracted features to assess whether the provided signal has been manipulated or combine the input with additional signals—biometric or not in nature—to estimate the likelihood of processing a real biometric signal.

Whether the captured biometric trait or an additional biometric signal is used to assess liveness is considered to be unimodal or multimodal liveness.

Unimodal

In this case, one or more features extracted from the biometric trait that is being processed are being analyzed to assess liveness. This can be either by analyzing a specific feature for indications of having been tampered with or look at the full raw input.

Examples:

- When performing a selfie-match, the liveness algorithm would look for reflections on the image which could indicate that the selfie wasn't taken from the live person, but by taking a picture on a computer screen.

- When analyzing the voice to perform an identity check, some algorithms check for background noise. If there's no background noise at all, this could mean that the voice has been generated artificially.

Multimodal

In contrast to liveness checks that are unimodal—based on one biometric modal—multimodal liveness tests extract features from additional biometric traits to assess the signal's integrity. In this case, a separate trait is being processed and (mis) alignments to the primary trait can be found.

If we use the example of a selfie match to analyze someone's face, a multimodal liveness check could include a behavioral biometric trait like how the person moves the mobile device they use to take the selfie. The movement sensors built into the device will be able to provide information on what movement the device detects.

... The absence of any movement can be a concerning signal for the liveness check... If the movement doesn't match to the selfie images collected by the camera, this can also be another red flag.

Furthermore, especially with unimodal liveness, implementations can also be differentiated between active and passive liveness checks.

CHAPTER 3   ADVERSARIAL BEHAVIOR—ATTACK AND DEFENSE

Active Liveness

One of the types of liveness methods is called "active liveness." This is when the user providing a biometric trait for login, or some other use, has to perform one or more instructed actions so the system can assess the integrity of the biometric signal.

If, for example, a bank requires a new customer to upload their selfie to check if it matches with the image of the driver's license they provided, an active liveness check could require them to follow instructions like facing in different directions, smile, tilt their head, etc.

Performing this check helps the application assess if the selfie has been pre-recorded or stolen. Having the person in front of the camera perform a set of randomized actions is a strong method to reduce the chance of impersonation. Attackers would have to produce the images in real time to succeed the liveness check, which would make the attack much more expensive.

The disadvantage of this approach is that active liveness requires people to understand and follow instructions. This makes the process longer and increases the risk of user fatigue or technical issues.

Passive Liveness

The objective of passive liveness is the same, but the approach is to extract information from the images or other sources without the user having to follow instructions. In the scenario of the selfie needed to verify the provided driver's license, passive liveness could consist of analyzing the picture for artifacts like reflections that indicate that the image was taken from a screen rather than from a live person.

Summary

This chapter provides the foundation for understanding the dynamics between attack and defense, by considering adversarial behavior, factors such as the cost of an attack, and methods used by biometric systems to keep secure. Liveness checks are a significant method of assessing the real-time presence of a live human being and for part of the defense of a biometric system.

This is the end of Part 1, in which we think about the growing use of biometrics, a structured way of conceptualizing how biometrics help us solve various problems, and how we can defend biometric systems against adversarial behavior. In Part 2, we go into detail about the use of various types of biometric data. Chapter 4 addresses physiological traits like fingerprints and retinas.

PART II

Sources of Biometric Signals

This is the end of Part 1, in which we think about the growing use of biometrics, a structured way of conceptualizing how biometrics help us solve various problems, and how we can defend biometric systems against adversarial behavior. In Part 2, we go into detail about the use of various types of biometric data. Chapter 4 addresses physiological traits like fingerprints and retinas.

In Part 2, we look at several sources of biometric data, approaching each source from the angle of considering what they are, the pros and cons of using them to solve particular problems, how the process works, and in what contexts they are currently being used. Part 2 is divided into four chapters: Physiological Characteristics, Variable Human Characteristics—Face, Behavioral Characteristics, and Voice.

CHAPTER 4

Physiological Characteristics

In this first chapter of Part 2, we present fingerprints, iris, retina, and DNA as sources of biometric data. We address what they are and how and in what contexts they are used. These sources of biometric data represent tangible, individual characteristics of our human body.

Did you know? If left on the right type of surface, fingerprints can stay for a very long time. Archaeologists have found fingerprints dating back as much as 80,000 years.[1]

Fingerprints

Perhaps the first source of biometric data that comes to mind for most people is fingerprints. As we have seen in Chapter 1, they were used as a method of identification thousands of years ago, and in the last 150 years they have been a greater and greater source of identification in forensic applications and now even more for the security of online accounts. In the following, we'll work toward a greater knowledge and understanding of this ubiquitous method of identification.

---

[1] Ancient fingerprints http://news.bbc.co.uk/1/hi/sci/tech/1766683.stm

CHAPTER 4   PHYSIOLOGICAL CHARACTERISTICS

What Are They?

From before birth, every person has a unique set of fingerprints based on the formation of ridges at the tip of our fingers. Fingerprints are formed before birth. At around the 12th week of gestation,[2] cells in the middle layer of the skin grow faster than those in the inner (basal) and outer layer. As the middle layer of skin creates extra cells, the skin buckles and ridges are formed. When a layer of keratin covers the skin between weeks 17 and 19, even more ridges are created. By the end of week 19, the fingerprint pattern is fixed.

Each fingerprint is made up of a combination of three types of patterns. These patterns are called arches, loops, and whorls.

Some factors that influence the formation of fingerprints are density of amniotic fluid, size of the fetus, and movement within the womb. As the formation of fingerprints is determined not only by genetics but a physiological process during gestation, not even identical twins possess the same fingerprint patterns.

Whenever we touch something, the patterns of our fingerprints can be left behind as either a layer of moisture and grease or an imprint on a material that is formed by the pressure of the finger and the ridges on the skin.

What Are Some Benefits and Drawbacks of Using Fingerprints?

- Although genetics have an influence on how the fingerprint patterns are created, even identical twins have unique patterns.

---

[2] How fingerprints are formed https://lozierinstitute.org/dive-deeper/when-and-how-fingerprints-form/.

- They stay the same over the whole life of a person. While fingerprints may be impacted or even lost by a cut, an abrasion, acid, or certain skin conditions, they usually recover within a month from these conditions.[3]

  As we age, our skin becomes less elastic and the ridges of our fingerprints get thicker. This doesn't change the pattern itself, but can make it harder to read the fingerprint correctly by taking a print.

- Fingerprints are a biometric trait that people can leave behind. When touching a surface, we leave behind a trace reflecting our fingerprints. Especially smooth and nonporous surfaces like Plexiglas make it easier for fingerprints to be taken after the fact.

- Removing fingerprints from the fingertips is a difficult task that often leads to even more distinguishing marks caused by the injuries induced by the procedure. The hand also offers additional identification marks such as the palm in cases where the fingerprint is inconclusive.

- They can be left at a previous time, thus not proving presence at the time in question. The strength of the science behind fingerprints can encourage people to draw illogical conclusions.

---

[3] Temporarily impacted or lost fingerprints www.sciencefocus.com/the-human-body/can-fingerprints-change-during-a-lifetime.

- Within the scientific community, there's still significant dispute about the legitimacy of using fingerprints to identify people. Numerous academics have pushed back on the narrative that fingerprints alone are adequate ways to identify individuals, especially for the purpose of crime identification. One reason for this is a lack of standardization when it comes to point counting and measurement of error rates.

- Other researchers have raised concerns that the presence of fingerprints during forensic investigations can distract from other information such as context.[4] The research indicates that forensic experts would, at times, be led to conclusions by over-indexing on the available evidence brought up by the fingerprints.[5]

In What Contexts Are They Used?

These days we encounter the use of fingerprints mainly for identification and authentication purposes. In recent years, it has become more and more common that smartphones, tablets, laptops, and other personal devices have a fingerprint sensor. The use of fingerprints is mainly limited to ensure exclusive access to our devices—unlock them—or to confirm transactions. In these cases, the fingerprint stays on the device and is not stored elsewhere.

---

[4] Fingerprints and objective forensics www.sciencedirect.com/science/article/abs/pii/S0379073805005876.
[5] Research: fingerprint can mislead www.sciencedirect.com/science/article/abs/pii/S0379073805005876.

There are other common uses of fingerprints as a biometric signal that are not part of most people's daily life. The use of fingerprints to identify people who were at a crime scene is one of them. Aside from attempting to identify the perpetrator of a crime, fingerprints can also be used to identify victims after natural or man-made disasters. This can be a way to identify victims instead of or in combination with other biometric signals like DNA.

Some countries require travelers to provide a fingerprint when entering the country or applying for a visa. In these cases, the fingerprints are matched with immigration data and/or Interpol's database to identify individuals that are either banned from entering the country or internationally wanted.

How Does It Work?

Most frequently these days, fingerprints are collected by scanning. Then they are either stored for future use or compared with previously scanned prints. Fingerprint sensors have become more widely available and have found their way into consumer products like smartphones, tablets, and laptops. We generally differentiate between Optical, Capacitive, and Ultrasonic fingerprint scanners[6]:

Optical Scanners

These types of fingerprint scanners take an image of the fingerprint by shining a light onto the finger and reflecting the light onto an image sensor. The image captured by the optical sensor is then translated into a digital signal to be processed.

Fingerprint scanners at airports are often optical scanners. They are increasingly being used in personal devices as well. An example of this is when the fingerprint scanner is integrated into a screen.

---

[6] Types of fingerprint scanners www.arrow.com/en/research-and-events/articles/how-fingerprint-sensors-work.

Capacitive Scanners

This is the type of fingerprint scanner we see more often in devices like smartphones and laptops. Just like a capacitive touchscreen, it works using human conductivity by creating an electrostatic field that then creates a digital image of the fingerprint. In order to capture all the details of a fingerprint, it breaks the surface into a tiny array of circuits. The position, size, and shape of the ridges changes the nature of the electrostatic field. The changes of this field are then translated into a digital signal to be processed.

Although this type of scanner is more expensive, it's also more secure due to the increased difficulty of bypassing it. If a replica of a human finger was used to attempt to bypass the fingerprint check, the electrostatic field would look significantly different.

Ultrasonic Scanners

Similar to how bats navigate in the dark, ultrasonic fingerprint scanners emit ultrasonic waves and then analyze the reflected waves to create a 3D map of the fingerprint. These types of scanners are currently being tested and may soon be placed behind the touchscreen of smartphones.[7]

Interesting Details About Fingerprints

It may not come as a surprise that the great apes, our closest relatives, also have fingerprints.[8] What is more surprising is that Koalas have them too. Given that Koalas' and humans' last common ancestors lived more than 100 million years ago, this commonality is likely due to similar circumstances taking place during evolution rather than genetic similarity.

---

[7] Ultrasonic fingerprint scanners www.lifewire.com/understanding-finger-scanners-4150464.

[8] Do Animals have fingerprints? www.newscientist.com/lastword/mg24933253-300-do-other-animals-have-fingerprints-and-what-purpose-do-they-serve/.

CHAPTER 4   PHYSIOLOGICAL CHARACTERISTICS

Scientists don't universally agree on the original purpose of fingerprints. One theory that there is significant speculation about is that fingerprints evolved as a result of climbing using the hands.

There are some rare conditions that lead to people not having fingerprints at all. One of them has the nickname "Immigration Delay Disease," which describes people's inability to perform biometric checks used at border crossings.[9] The scientific name of this rare condition is Adermatoglyphia.

Iris

Two different parts of the eye provide useful biometric data. We'll start by discussing the one we notice almost immediately when meeting someone—the iris.

What Are They?

The iris is the colored part of our eye. It serves the purpose of controlling the amount of light allowed into the eye. Similar to fingerprints, the iris develops during pregnancy. A bit sooner than fingerprints, their development begins at week 7 of gestation.[10] A combination of genetics and environmental factors in the womb shape the iris into its unique visible pattern.

The iris is made up of an inner layer called the iris pigment epithelium and an outer layer called the stroma. In the middle are dilator and sphincter muscles that control the size of the pupil.

---

[9] "Immigration Delay Disease" www.jaad.org/article/S0190-9622(09)01475-3/fulltext.

[10] Iris during pregnancy www.babycentre.co.uk/a25040510/fetal-development-your-babys-eyes-and-sight.

CHAPTER 4   PHYSIOLOGICAL CHARACTERISTICS

What characteristics make them suitable?

- Each iris is unique and distinguishable from all others. Not only do identical twins have distinct iris patterns, even the left and right iris of the same person are different from each other.

- Being externally visible, the unique pattern of the iris can be picked up using a basic camera. This contributes to its ease of use as a biometric signal.

- Compared with fingerprints, the iris has the benefit of being covered by the cornea. This prevents dirt, debris or physical damage from causing inconclusive scanning results.

In What Contexts Are They Used?

The use of irises as a biometric signal hasn't entered the consumer space as much as fingerprints, face recognition, or voice-based biometrics. Currently, it's mostly used by law enforcement agencies as a supplement for other biometrics to identify people.[11]

How Does It Work?

A high-resolution image of a person's iris is matched against images stored in a database. The ability to identify enough details from a picture to perform effective matching of the iris depends on the number of pixels that

---

[11] Use of Iris www.biometricsinstitute.org/types-of-biometrics-eye-iris-use-cases.

can be captured by the camera covering the desired area. A minimum of 70 pixels in a radius is considered necessary to capture the details of a human iris.[12] Most systems operate with a range of 80–130 pixels.

Interesting Details About Irises

There are various theories and research activity to tie the characteristics of the iris to the detection or prediction of health concerns. One of the theories is called Iridology, which is a technique where properties of the iris can be used to assess an individual's health.[13] This technique is not yet widely researched and lacks broad support from scientists and medical professionals.

Retina

Often confused with the iris, the retina is another part of our eyes that has a unique pattern. As with fingerprints and the pattern of the iris, not even identical twins have the same pattern of blood vessels in their retinas.

What Are They?

The retina is a layer of nerve tissue at the back of the eye that has a unique pattern of blood vessels. It is the layer through which all light coming into our eyes passes for conversion into electrical signals before being sent along the optical nerve to our brain.[14] The numerous blood vessels located in the retina make it look mostly red or orange.

---

[12] Iris resolution—www.robots.ox.ac.uk/~az/lectures/est/iris.pdf.
[13] Iridology—www.allaboutvision.com/eye-care/eye-exams/what-is-iridology/.
[14] Retina—https://medlineplus.gov/ency/article/002291.htm.

CHAPTER 4   PHYSIOLOGICAL CHARACTERISTICS

What characteristics make them suitable?

- The structure of the capillaries that ensure proper blood flow to the retina is unique.
- Can't be picked up with a picture, so more difficult to steal.
- Tricking an access system is difficult as the retina is almost impossible to reproduce.
- The retina decays very quickly after a person dies, which makes extracting it from a corpse a useless endeavor.[15]
- Medical conditions such as diabetes or glaucoma can alter the structure of the retinal blood vessels, otherwise it stays stable during the lifespan of the eye.
- As the scan uses the reflection cast by the infrared light, there's no digital image of the retina to be stored. This can cut down on privacy risks, but also complicates the auditing process.
- Unlike the iris, the retina can't be seen from the outside, which requires special equipment to analyze it.
- This procedure is more complex than the scan of an iris and takes longer to perform. In contrast to an iris scan, a retinal scan has to be performed closer to the person's eye and can be influenced by health conditions mentioned previously.

---

[15] Retina after death—www.techtarget.com/whatis/definition/retina-scan.

CHAPTER 4   PHYSIOLOGICAL CHARACTERISTICS

In What Contexts Are They Used?

Retina scanners are often used in high-security environments to ensure access is limited to the right people. It can be used as a highly secure biometric signal in military bases, nuclear reactors, and other high-security locations.

There are also medical use cases that benefit from scanning the retina. While the pattern of the retinal blood vessels typically stays the same during the entire life, there are some medical conditions that can alter it.

Doctors tend to perform retina scans if they observe symptoms of conditions such as diabetes or macular degeneration.[16] Both of these conditions impact the retinal blood vessels and can be diagnosed by analyzing retinal scans.

How Does It Work?

Retina scanners cast an invisible beam of low-energy infrared light onto a person's retina and create a picture of the pattern of blood vessels,[17] which then is translated into a digital map that can be compared to a previously stored model of the retina. Scanning the retina is a relatively slow process and takes around 30 seconds and an eyepiece must be worn. This process makes scanning the retina less convenient than taking a picture of an iris.

DNA

The least tangible, though most ubiquitous of the anatomical sources of biometric data, DNA can be found in almost every part of the body, including skin cells, body fluids, and hair.

---

[16] Retina—Medical use cases www.webmd.com/eye-health/what-is-retinal-imaging.

[17] Retina scanners www.biometricupdate.com/201307/explainer-retinal-scan-technology.

CHAPTER 4   PHYSIOLOGICAL CHARACTERISTICS

What Is It?

Deoxyribonucleic acid (DNA) is the hereditary information contained in each of our cells. It forms a unique string of information defining the way each organism develops and functions. DNA is stored in a similar way software code is stored. It consists of Billions of data points made up by adenine (A), guanine (G), cytosine (C), and thymine (T).

What characteristics make it suitable?

- It's one of the few types of biometric data that can be "left behind" by the person.

- DNA is the only biometric information that allows related people to be linked to each other.

- The structure of DNA is almost "digital," thus making it easier to compare samples.

- DNA provides a lot of information that can identify a person but also points out certain health risks.

- While each person has a unique set of genetic information, there are no applications where this is used for authentication or access control, since testing is a more elaborate, expensive, and time-consuming procedure than using other biometric traits for such tasks.

In What Contexts Is It Used?

Forensics is the use of science in a legal context. Matching DNA to a specific person is often used to identify criminals. Forensic investigators look for traces that contain DNA at crime scenes. DNA can be found in hair, skin, blood, semen, saliva, or bacteria left behind by people who were at the location a crime took place.

CHAPTER 4   PHYSIOLOGICAL CHARACTERISTICS

If forensic scientists want to determine who has been in a specific room recently, they search for anything that contains DNA information. This would indicate how many different people have likely been in said room and then allow them to compare the DNA with available data to identify the individuals.

In the field of healthcare, DNA analysis is mostly used to identify risk factors and to aid in the diagnosis for inherited diseases.

Genealogy tests have become more and more popular lately. They allow people to trace their ancestry and find relatives who have also done the tests.

How Does It Work?

Perhaps the most technologically complex of the methods of biometric analysis, processing and analyzing DNA is an expensive and time-consuming process. Once a sample is collected, the DNA must be isolated from the sample. The DNA is then examined. Once all relevant information is extracted, it will then be compared with DNA from a known person.

Interesting Details About DNA

Red blood cells have no nuclear DNA. Hair, if cut, has no DNA, though DNA can be retrieved from the root of the hair.

99.9% of our DNA code is the same among all human beings. The 0.1% that varies makes up for our differences. In fact, humans and bananas are more than 60% identical.[18]

---

[18] www.pfizer.com/news/articles/how_genetically_related_are_we_to_bananas#:~:text=Banana%3A%20more%20than%2060%20percent,(including%20bananas)%20and%20animals.

CHAPTER 4 PHYSIOLOGICAL CHARACTERISTICS

Most National or International DNA databases are maintained and used for forensic purposes. The first National DNA database was created in the UK in 1995.[19] One of the supporting arguments to build and maintain these types of databases are based on studies that a majority of crimes are being committed by repeat offenders. Based on this, criminals—of different levels—are being added to these DNA databases.

Summary

Physiological biometric traits like fingerprints, iris, retina, and DNA are characteristics that reflect the way our body is made or appears. Due to factors like inheritance and the physical process before and after birth, they are strong signals that help identify people or assess health.

Aside from explaining what these characteristics are and how they can provide useful biometric data, this chapter also shows some interesting details about these sources.

In Chapter 5, we go into greater depth about facial recognition as a biometric tool.

---

[19] First national DNA database www.sciencedirect.com/topics/medicine-and-dentistry/dna-database.

CHAPTER 5

Variable Human Characteristics—Face

This chapter takes an in-depth look at face-based biometrics—a complex process where detected faces are compared to existing models for identification, authentication, or other types of analysis. Just as a friend recognizes you by your face, face-based biometrics use the unique features of your face for recognition, identification, and authentication.

We consider what makes facial analysis an appropriate method of identification and authentication and explore the diverse applications of face-based biometrics, from unlocking smartphones to bolstering security systems. We discuss how this technology functions and uncover its strengths and weaknesses.

What Characteristics Make the Face a Suitable Biometric Trait?

Faces make for excellent biometric traits due to their unique and stable characteristics, which are ideal for reliable identification and valuable health assessments. Each face is a complex mosaic of features—the distances between eyes, the shape of the cheekbones, the contour of the jawline, and the intricacies of the eye, nose, and mouth structures. These features are distinct to each individual and, importantly, remain relatively consistent over time, even as a person ages. This constancy allows for accurate long-term identification, a critical aspect in security and personal verification systems.

Additionally, subtle changes in facial features can be indicative of health conditions, making faces not just tools for identification but also for potential health monitoring and diagnosis.

The non-invasive nature of facial recognition further adds to its utility, providing a seamless and efficient means of gathering biometric data.

In What Contexts Are They Used?

Faces as biometric signals are utilized in a diverse range of contexts, each leveraging the unique capability of facial recognition technology. Here's an overview of different areas where face-based biometrics play a pivotal role:

Identification and Authentication

Commonly used for personal identification and security authentication, facial recognition is integral in systems like Apple's FaceID, which Apple introduced in iPhones in 2017. This technology verifies a user's identity to unlock devices or access services, ensuring that only authorized individuals gain entry.

Other situations where our faces are used to identify our identity or authenticate us to allow access to a system or facility happen when we sign up for financial services that require a KYC (Know Your Customer) process or when we pass immigration at an airport.

Amazon X-Ray on Prime Video

Do you ever pause a movie to do a deep dive about an actor you've just seen? Amazon has you covered. An innovative application of facial recognition is seen in Amazon's X-Ray feature on Prime Video. This system uses facial recognition to identify actors on screen by comparing detected faces against a database of actor images, like those on IMDb. Amazon's Rekognition API performs this by analyzing video images and returning information about the recognized celebrities with a confidence score.

Security Cameras and Surveillance

In the realm of public safety and security, facial recognition technology is employed in security cameras and surveillance systems. It assists in monitoring public spaces, identifying persons of interest, and enhancing overall security infrastructure.

Security cameras have evolved from just recording video feeds so they can be manually reviewed when needed. They increasingly have capabilities to detect faces, and run recognition algorithms on them. Deployments of more sophisticated security camera systems can take place on private premises like company campuses, retail stores, or in the public space. These deployments can cause significant controversy due to privacy concerns and fear of misuse of the collected data.

Home Security

For personal home security systems, facial recognition can add an extra layer of protection, allowing systems to distinguish between known occupants and strangers, and alerting homeowners accordingly. As stated in the introductory chapter of this book, the adoption of video-enabled door-bells is just one example of cameras being deployed in the residential space.

This wide array of applications demonstrates the versatility and breadth of facial recognition technology, making it a valuable tool in various domains from entertainment to personal and public security. With that, risks and concerns on how the widespread adoption of facial recognition impacts the privacy of individuals in the private and public spaces arise.

CHAPTER 5   VARIABLE HUMAN CHARACTERISTICS—FACE

How Does It Work?

It's a blend of two core processes: face detection and face recognition.

How Face Detection Works

Face detection involves analyzing still or moving images to detect the presence of faces. Products that use this, often indicate the presence of one or multiple faces with markers, such as bright green squares. This is often seen in digital cameras, photo apps on smartphones, and video- or image-editing software. This stage does not involve identifying or creating individual profiles, but rather, it's about recognizing the presence of a face in the image.

Face detection algorithms scan images for patterns that match typical facial features, such as the eyes, nose, and mouth. Modern systems are quite advanced and can detect faces from various angles and in different lighting conditions. They look for contrasts and shapes that resemble human faces, which is why sometimes, they might mistakenly identify objects with face-like features.

How Recognition Works

Once a face is detected, the recognition process can begin. This involves analyzing specific facial features—distances between eyes, the shape of the cheekbones, or the contour of the jawline. These measurements can be compared against a database of known faces to find a match. This comparison is not just about matching images; it's about understanding the geometry of a face and its unique characteristics.

Sources of Images and 2D vs. 3D Mapping

Face detection and recognition can work with various sources of images, including photographs, video feeds, and live cameras. The process can operate using simple 2D images, like those taken with a standard camera. Some systems use 3D facemaps, where a 2D image is enhanced with depth information. This is achieved using additional sensors or algorithms that add a three-dimensional perspective, making the recognition process more accurate and less prone to errors and more robust to attempts to trick the system with the use of printed images.

In summary, while face detection and recognition are part of the same family of technologies, they provide distinct values. Detection is about finding faces in images, while recognition is about matching those faces to identities. Both processes are integral to the expanding field of face-based biometrics.

Developer Integration

Building facial recognition software is an expensive process that requires specialized skills, expensive infrastructure to train the model, and is very time intensive. Most developers don't build these abilities themselves.

Various resources are available for developers to integrate facial recognition into their applications, expanding the technology's use into numerous custom applications.

Client-Side and Server-Side Biometrics in Facial Recognition

In the realm of facial recognition, biometric data can be stored and/or processed in two main environments: on the device (client-side) and on a server (server-side), each offering benefits, risks, and applications.

Client-Side Biometrics

On the client side, facial recognition typically occurs directly on a user's device, such as a smartphone or personal computer. This approach is often used for device unlocking or application authentication. The facial data is processed and stored locally, which can lead to quicker response times and potentially enhanced privacy, as the biometric information doesn't leave the device. However the accuracy can be lower due to the limitations of how much computing power the device has. It also doesn't allow the face to be compared to a centrally stored template to continuously ensure the actual identity of a person.

Server-Side Biometrics

Conversely, server-side facial recognition processes and/or stores biometric data on remote servers or cloud-based platforms. This method is more commonly used in situations where a face needs to be compared to a template available from a different source. It offers the advantage of more powerful processing capabilities, potentially leading to greater accuracy and the ability to handle large databases of facial data.

Server-side processing is essential for applications requiring high assurance, such as in banking or access to sensitive data in corporate environments. However, it raises concerns about data privacy and the security of biometric data during transmission and storage.

Both client-side and server-side facial recognition have their places in the biometric landscape, with the choice between them often depending on the specific requirements of security, speed, and data privacy of the application in question. Some integrations use a mix of these two elements to improve the balance between performance, privacy, and assurance.

Strengths and Weaknesses of Facial biometrics

Strengths of Facial Biometrics

Faces are a universal biometric marker, making this technology applicable to almost everyone, thereby ensuring versatility and inclusivity.

Comprehensive Data Points

Facial recognition technology analyzes a variety of detailed facial features, such as the distances between eyes, forehead to chin, nose to mouth, and the depth and shape of eye sockets, cheekbones, lips, ears, and chin. This creates a rich, multidimensional dataset for precise identification.

Technological Advancements in Cameras

The high-resolution imaging offered by modern cameras, especially in smartphones and tablets, significantly enhances the accuracy and reliability of facial recognition systems.

Prevalence of Cameras

The widespread availability of front-facing cameras in consumer electronics has made facial recognition more accessible and mainstream.

User Familiarity and Comfort

With its growing use in everyday technology like phone unlocking and customer service, users have become more accustomed to and comfortable with face-based biometrics.

Non-Invasive and Real-Time Processing

Facial recognition is non-invasive, making it user-friendly, and it allows for real-time identification and verification.

Weaknesses of Facial Biometrics

Lack of Secrecy

Faces are publicly visible and can be captured without consent. This is particularly driven by the increased presence of cameras and publicly available images.

Especially for people with significant online presences, this can put them at higher risk of their facial biometrics being abused for impersonation attacks.

AI-Generated Spoofs

Advances in AI (Artificial Intelligence) technologies have enabled the creation of realistic deepfakes and synthetic images, posing significant security threats to face recognition systems.

The speed in which these tools are improving can't be accurately described on a medium like a book. At the time of writing these books, countless products and technologies have been made available at no or little cost to people to use sophisticated AI algorithms that can create high-quality images based on text-input or reference-images. The cost of reproducing convincing artificial images is rapidly decreasing.

Diversity and Bias Issues

The effectiveness of facial recognition can vary across different ethnicities and ages, highlighting concerns about fairness and reliability. Continuous research is required to address these issues.

Challenges in Varying Conditions

Facial recognition can be less effective in poor lighting or when the face undergoes changes due to aging, makeup, or surgery, affecting its reliability.

Search Engines for Faces

To make this concept more tangible, we'd like to use an example with real-world use. This example can also be applied to other identifiable biometric traits like voice, gait, etc. The easier the trait can be collected and broader the availability, the more attractive such a search engine could be. Given the prevalence of the visual traces we leave online, it's not a surprise that face-based matching is a viable implementation.

What if someone could search for all of my images using an image of my face?

If I perform an image search on Google or Bing on my name, I will receive a number of images that based on public records have been linked to my name. Some of them show me, others show people with the same name, and others show something else. While said link between my image and (real world) identity can already break down silos and lead to privacy issues, it still relies on information having been linked to the source of the images.

The step that would have a more drastic impact on the basic concept of privacy is when someone can take a picture of my face and have a search engine provide other pictures of me, even if there's no link to my name or other identifying information being provided.

Batman was able to use such technology in his Batmobile. There are examples of real world deployments that provide this functionality.

CHAPTER 5   VARIABLE HUMAN CHARACTERISTICS—FACE

Face Search for Law Enforcement

One of these examples is a US-based technology company called Clearview.[1] Clearview provides their service to police departments and allows them to upload images of suspects and receive matching results from the vast—likely billions—number of pictures they have obtained from various online-sources.

Clearview is an interesting example of how a technology breaks expectations of privacy. There's a lot of research and reporting about this case, given its potential implications on how law enforcement conducts their work, with concerns of accuracy and transparency. In 2023, Kashmir Hill released a book called "Your Face Belongs To Us"[2] where Clearview is at the center of her reporting on how facial recognition can break down the fragmentation of our data.

Face Search for Consumers

Rather than doing an image search based on text, or searching for a specific picture, face-search-engines look for pictures of the same person.

We're going to refrain from naming the specific tools we used for the experiments due to the potential privacy issues the use of these tools can have and to make it clear that we're not endorsing any of them in this book.

I used a good-quality image I took of myself recently, that is also available online. The tool suggested that I upload multiple pictures of myself for better results. The first time I used it I ignored this suggestion, because I didn't want to provide them with more images (not necessarily a rational decision). Even when using a free version, I received 34 results right away. Some of the images were taken almost 20 years ago.

---

[1] Clearview www.clearview.ai/.
[2] Your Face belongs to us www.simonandschuster.co.uk/books/Your-Face-Belongs-to-Us/Kashmir-Hill/9781398509177.

75

CHAPTER 5   VARIABLE HUMAN CHARACTERISTICS—FACE

- Two versions were the same pictures cropped
- One was my face, among other faces, on a video-conference call where the screenshot was used for an article about said call.
- The most surprising ones were images where I was part of a larger group at business or social events.

In some cases, the paid version showed more results or provided the link to where it found these images. A part of the results I got for my image were profile pictures, which wasn't a surprise as they tend to get scraped (automatically gathered) by a lot of apps. Kashmir Hill—author of "Your Face Belongs To Us"—describes how Clearview fetched Millions of profile images from Venmo, a payment application, for example.

Setting alerts: In some cases, these tools offer an alerting feature for when a new image of said person appears in their database. While there can be legitimate use cases if used by the person the face "belongs" to, there are as many—if not more—ways this could be abused by people with ill intentions.

Accuracy and False Positives

Most of these face-search engines include a disclaimer that their search results may not be perfect and note that "some people look alike." I conducted a few searches using pictures from the website thispersondoesnotexist.com,[3] a site that uses Artificial intelligence to generate random images of people. The fact that all of the face-searches resulted in dozens of results from these faces that don't exist is also telling how the people building them tend to show results even when their algorithms have low confidence. A (paying) user might not enjoy the tool if no results come back.

---

[3] thispersondoesnotexist.com https://thispersondoesnotexist.com/.

Good Intentions

The companies building these types of face-search engines certainly do this with good intentions. Clearview's stated mission is:[4] "... is to create and deliver identification technology that helps combat crime and fraud, keep communities safe and industry and commerce secure, protect victims and promote justice." Providing law enforcement officers the ability to reduce the time to identify a suspect in itself can be considered a net positive for our society. Companies like Clearview argue that by limiting access to their technology to accredited organizations, the risk of abuse is acceptable.

Other products that are accessible to a broader audience often claim that they provide power to victims of stalking or leaked personal images by providing them with insight in what images are shared where.

This paragraph is not meant to justify all these efforts, and the proverb that "the road to hell is paved with good intentions" might be applicable here.

Clearview is not the only company with these capabilities. In recent years, other attempts have been made to build "face-search-engines" with varied levels of success. The technology is available and products like these are currently in production.

While Clearview only sells to accredited law enforcement organizations, this is a choice others may make differently.

Summary

Facial recognition has vast potential in security and identification as well as inherent challenges, from privacy concerns to technological limitations. All of this underscores the need for balanced and ethical application.

---

[4] Clearview mission www.clearview.ai/principles.

CHAPTER 5 VARIABLE HUMAN CHARACTERISTICS—FACE

Chapter 5 takes a deep dive into the use and limitations of facial recognition technology. We see various contexts in which it is proving useful and some challenges to its correct use. We consider the risks and challenges associated with face-based biometrics, including the accuracy of algorithms and the potential for false positives in various scenarios.

Typing patterns and walking patterns as well as other types of movement and behavior are increasingly used in biometric systems. In Chapter 6, we look at a different variety of characteristics used in the field of biometrics, namely, behavioral biometrics.

CHAPTER 6

Behavioral Characteristics

As opposed to the physiological characteristics used in other biometric traits like fingerprints, retina scans, and facial recognition, behavioral biometrics are characteristics derived from the way we consciously use our bodies. This type of biometric evaluation focuses on dynamic patterns, habits, and how we interact with technology, rather than fixed physiological attributes.

The line between physiological and behavioral characteristics is not always solid. Many biometric traits blend physiological and behavioral elements to some extent, and the balance of these components can vary. For instance, while many vocal characteristics stem from habitual use, some voice characteristics are shaped by the physical aspects of the voice box or vocal cords. Thus, whether a biometric system is labeled as behavioral or physiological sometimes depends on which features are extracted. The voice is a good example of a trait that consists of multiple behavioral features that are influenced but not defined by anatomical characteristics.

A wide range of behavioral traits can be used for biometrics. In this chapter, we will address typing patterns, walking patterns, and other movements and behavior.

CHAPTER 6   BEHAVIORAL CHARACTERISTICS

Typing Patterns

The way we type on a physical keyboard or how we use a touchscreen is a behavioral biometric we may notice being used more and more. While some people have mastered touch typing—using all ten fingers to type on a keyboard—we all still have distinct patterns in which we hit the keys. How are these patterns assessed? As we will see with voice, creating a template of someone's typing patterns involves measuring several variables. A writing pattern can be comprehensively described by considering the following characteristics:

- **Press-release timing**: This is based on measurements of the timing of when each key is pressed and then released. The rhythm and pace at which someone types can be distinctive.

- **Flight Time**: The flight time refers to the duration between releasing one key and pressing the next. It measures the pause someone typically makes as they move their fingers from one key to another.

- **Dwell Time**: The amount of time a key is held down can vary from person to person. Some people press keys quickly, barely touching them, while others hold keys down longer.

- **Error Patterns**: This refers to the frequency and types of errors made while typing. The subsequent corrections of these errors are also a characteristic of an individual's typing pattern.

- **Typing Speed**: This relates to the average speed a person types. Temporary changes in speed, depending on the complexity of text, can also be significant.

- **Typing Rhythm:** The consistency and variation in rhythm while typing complete sentences or single strings of characters like passwords or names.

- **Pressure Sensitivity:** How hard a key is pressed can also be a distinctive feature.

How Does It Work?

The way we press and release the keys on a keyboard generates a range of metrics and characteristics. Here, the keyboard acts as a sensor, with each key detecting two states: pressed and unpressed. Some mechanical keyboards can also measure the speed and pressure with which keys are pressed. To create the template for an individual's typing pattern, they are typically asked to type a specific text—this could be a set passage, their password, or simply free-form text. By analyzing keystroke dynamics such as those listed previously, an algorithm can develop a template that captures the unique aspects of how someone types. This template can then be used for comparison in future sessions to evaluate the likelihood that the person typing is who they claim to be or to monitor how their typing pattern evolves.

In What Contexts Are They Used?

The most prominent use case for this type of biometrics is to identify someone or to grant permission.

Authentication at login time

Companies like TypingDNA[1] offer solutions that analyze the typing pattern of password entries. This is done to assess if they match the user's previously created templates. This method can be implemented very

---

[1] www.typingdna.com/.

broadly—from using the patterns while typing the password as a second factor to using it for account recovery if the user has lost access to their credentials.

Continuous authentication

There is a growing focus in research on how keystroke dynamics can be used to perform continuous authentication. This entails constantly assessing if the person typing is still the legitimate actor or if someone else got hold of the device.

Vendors like TypinDNA have launched products in that space that allow enterprises to continuously assess the identity of their workforce.

Sentiment analysis

Interesting research[2] was conducted at Gdansk University of Technology in Poland which indicates that keystroke dynamics can give insights into the sentiments of the user. Participants were asked to write about positive and negative experiences. The analysis of keystroke dynamics led to classification with accuracy slightly higher than random. Though this procedure is far from foolproof, it represents a promising start in the use of typing patterns for sentiment analysis.

Limitations

Risk of error, need for balance. Deciding what decisions will be made using typing patterns. Perhaps a need to layer with other methods.

Like all biometric systems, typing patterns are probabilistic in nature. This means that any identity verification based on typing dynamics should be considered an assumption made with varying degrees of confidence. No matter how sophisticated the technology is, there is an inherent trade-off between false positives (incorrectly verifying an unauthorized person) and false negatives (failing to recognize an authorized person).

---

[2] Research sentiment based on typing patterns—www.ncbi.nlm.nih.gov/pmc/articles/PMC8434638/.

The acceptable threshold for these errors must be carefully set based on the required level of accuracy for each application. This balance is crucial, as it impacts both the security and usability of the system, necessitating ongoing adjustments to maintain optimal performance.

Privacy and Legal Risks

Although typing pattern data does not typically involve any information that would fall under medical or health-related categories, and it can often be anonymized, there are still significant privacy and legal risks. The implementation of true privacy-preserving anonymization is not a trivial task. Research[3] has shown how data aggregation, a form of data anonymization for keystroke data, still leaves privacy concerns.

The collection of typing patterns necessarily involves capturing the actual content typed by a person to analyze timings such as flight time and keystroke dynamics. This requirement raises concerns, particularly when the data is processed by third parties. In such scenarios, it is crucial to obtain user consent.

Even the application of an anonymization mechanism like data aggregation can still bear significant privacy risks. In certain jurisdictions, even recording the content of what someone types without explicit permission could be classified as wiretapping. This highlights the importance of careful legal compliance and robust privacy safeguards in the use of typing biometrics.

---

[3] Information leakage after data aggregation https://f005.backblazeb2.com/file/nyitlamp/papers/JCS-2018.pdf.

CHAPTER 6   BEHAVIORAL CHARACTERISTICS

Walking Patterns/Gait Recognition

Another behavioral biometric modality is called gait recognition or the identification of walking patterns. Due to physiological and behavioral reasons, each individual has a distinct way of walking. A combination of characteristics related to gait can be turned into a biometric template.

Walking patterns are created by measuring a list of characteristics such as:

- **Stride Length and Speed**: Measures the length of each step and the speed at which a person walks.

- **Cadence**: Closely related to stride length and speed, cadence refers to the rate at which a person takes steps, usually expressed in steps per minute.

- **Posture**: Observes the general stance and positioning of the body when walking, including the tilt of the torso and the swing of the arms.

- **Motion of Limbs**: Analyzes specific movements of the legs and arms when walking.

- **Foot Dynamics**: Looks at how the foot strikes the ground, the angle of motion, and the force distribution.

CHAPTER 6   BEHAVIORAL CHARACTERISTICS

How Does It Work?[4]

Gait recognition typically entails analyzing a sequence of frames that capture a person walking. An algorithm processes these frames to create a simplified digital skeleton, typically mapping the spine and legs as overlays on the moving image. This skeletal model helps measure specific gait characteristics, such as stride length, speed, and limb motion. When these metrics are combined, it forms a distinctive gait pattern for each individual. This pattern can then be used to create a new template or be compared against existing templates to verify identity. In theory, this allows for the identification of individuals based on their unique walking patterns, providing a non-invasive biometric solution that can be implemented from a distance.

---

[4] Digital Skeleton Illustration—Illustration generated with DALL-E.

CHAPTER 6   BEHAVIORAL CHARACTERISTICS

A newer field of research[5] is gait recognition based on accelerometer data collected from a smartwatch or smartphone. Where image data is traditionally used to create a gait pattern, in this space the accelerometer—a sensor that can measure linear acceleration based on vibration, which is found in most modern smartphones—is used to collect relevant data. The advantage of this approach is that the sensor is carried wherever the person goes without the need for a line of sight from complex camera systems.

Limitations

Several specific limitations make the collection and analysis of walking patterns more challenging and potentially less effective than other biometric methods. As with all biometric systems, gait recognition is not an exact science. Each captured sequence varies slightly, and the algorithm must match these variations against the closest existing template, which is inherently probabilistic.

One of the challenges of gait analysis is that the measurements from one person to the next will be relatively close together. Considering that most grown individual's height falls within a relatively small range, we are dealing with slight differences between subjects. The requirements for the precision of assessing gait are very high.

The equipment required for high-quality gait analysis is also specialized and costly. Accurate gait extraction requires high-resolution cameras and high frame-rate video capture, conditions which are compounded by suboptimal outdoor lighting that can significantly degrade image quality. Additionally, the angle and perspective of the camera are crucial as variations in camera angle can lead to significant discrepancies in measurements, reducing the reliability of the system.

---

[5] Accelerometer based gait recognition—https://citeseerx.ist.psu.edu/document?doi=09e44ed1eee758c84ba7300bf9596601678c30a6.

CHAPTER 6   BEHAVIORAL CHARACTERISTICS

Precise feature extraction and subsequent identification depend on consistent positioning. Because it requires off-body cameras, camera-based gait recognition is not a workable authentication method. The use of gait pattern for (continuous) authentication is the subject of research where smartphone accelerometers are used.

In What Contexts Are They Used?

Due to the complexities involved in setting up the necessary camera systems, gait analysis is predominantly utilized in specialized fields. One significant application is in **medical diagnostics**, where it helps detect and treat various conditions. For instance, children with cerebral palsy can benefit from gait analysis, which is used to improve their movement control through tailored treatments. There are also deployments[6] that can provide early detections and an in-depth analysis of degenerative joint disease osteoarthritis—the most common form of arthritis.

Additionally, **athletic training** often incorporates regular gait analysis to identify movement patterns that could potentially lead to injuries or long-term complications, thus helping athletes prevent these issues.

In the realm of **security and surveillance**, gait analysis has seen broader applications due to advancements in video camera coverage, image quality, and processing power. Notably, reports from 2018 have highlighted its use in China, where the government has begun deploying gait recognition technologies across its extensive network of surveillance cameras to identify individuals in public spaces.

---

[6] Arthritis detection with camera-based gait recognition https://embassies.gov.il/la/AboutIsrael/AboutIsraelInfo/Pages/Gait-analysis-made-easy.aspx.

CHAPTER 6   BEHAVIORAL CHARACTERISTICS

Other Movement and Behavior

There are varying degrees of research and use for several other traits with a high degree of behavioral characteristics. Here, we will briefly discuss some interesting examples.

Hand movement, orientation, and grasp[7]

This is the observation of movement and grasp patterns with accelerometers and gyroscopes. This approach, combined with other metrics, is proposed for use as continuous authentication of users of devices such as smartphones and smartwatches.

Eye tracking (Gaze[8]**)**

Eye tracking analyzes the movement of the eye to assess the user's intent to interact with a device. A paper from the University of Delaware and the College of William and Mary also proposes the use of this method to input authentication details to access smartphones.

Swipe patterns[9] **on touchscreens**

Build and compare models based on the characteristics of using a touch device.

Mouse dynamics[10]

Patterns of use of a computer mouse.

Interaction[11] **with User Interfaces**

Use of patterns when people interact with a user interface, tracking of usual or unusual activity.

Signature Dynamics

---

[7] hand movement https://scholarworks.wm.edu/cgi/viewcontent.cgi?article=1734&context=aspubs.
[8] gaze tracking https://dongshuhao.github.io/assets/pdf/2015/Liu2015.pdf.
[9] swipe patterns https://arxiv.org/pdf/1207.6231.pdf.
[10] mouse dynamics https://ieeexplore.ieee.org/abstract/document/4288179.
[11] Interaction with user interface https://docs.lib.purdue.edu/dissertations/AAI3291194/.

CHAPTER 6 BEHAVIORAL CHARACTERISTICS

Detection of Device Possession Change

Organizations and consumers often struggle with protecting sensitive data accessible from stolen devices like smartphones or laptops. A common way to reduce the risk of data theft by someone who stole a device is to require regular re-authentication—for example, having to enter the password once a day to continue an established session. This isn't the best user experience. This also leaves a window for up to 23 hours and 59 minutes during which a thief could use a stolen device to access sensitive data. While modern security systems analyze dozens if not hundreds of signals to assess the possibility of a device having been stolen, factors attributed to behavioral biometrics haven't been taken into context.

A research paper published in 2024[12] describes ways to assess whether a smartphone is still in possession of the legitimate owner. SMARTCOPE stands for Smartphone Change of Possession Evaluation. In order to detect abnormalities in the patterns of behavioral biometric traits like touchscreen swipe patterns, signals from the accelerometer and gyroscope of the device, and other biometric traits, evaluation for continuous authentication is a framework. *If said signals have changed significantly enough, a risk alert could be issued triggering a re-authentication or even (temporarily) locking access to the device or certain resources.*

This is a good example of how layering multiple behavioral biometric traits, that isolated might not allow for a robust conclusion, can provide a more holistic signal on which a user-visible action can be triggered.

---

[12] Smartcope paper—https://files.nyit-lamp.com/file/nyitlamp/papers/cariello2023smartcope.pdf.

CHAPTER 6 BEHAVIORAL CHARACTERISTICS

Concept Drift

One effect that impacts the accuracy of behavioral biometric traits over time is called concept drift. This describes changes in the patterns over time.

- **Long-term shift** describes changes happening over the time frame of months or years. It often comes from gradual changes in human behavior which can result from aging, physical health challenges, evolving habits, or changes in the use of technology. Proficiency like improvements in typing skills can also cause a long-term shift, making the trait less accurate when used for authentication/identification purposes.

- **Short-term shifts** happen within much shorter time frames. Influencing factors such as mood, fatigue, or stress can influence changes in behavioral traits within minutes or hours.

To prevent drift from negatively impacting the quality of the data, drift detection algorithms[13] are put in place. They attempt to detect concept drift and adjust the output to keep the accuracy of the classifier intact.

Prevalence of Use

Unlike most physiological traits like fingerprints, face recognition, etc., the use of behavioral modalities or features is in many cases still in the research phase. Especially in consumer applications, real-world deployments that rely on behavioral traits are relatively rare.

---

[13] Drift detection algorithm www.sciencedirect.com/science/article/abs/pii/S0952197620303729.

The use of behavioral traits is also, per their nature, less visible for everyday use of devices and technologies.

The most prevalent trait of this family is certainly voice, where everyday deployments such as voice-based assistants like Siri, Google Assistant, etc. have become widespread and the use of our voice is a factor of identification.

Summary

Behavioral biometrics analyze patterns in how individuals interact with technology, such as typing rhythms, mouse usage, and gait. These traits are less invasive and observe dynamic behaviors rather than fixed physiological attributes. Concept drift, where behavior changes over time, affects accuracy. Typing patterns, for example, involve timing, speed, and error frequency. While useful for authentication, they pose privacy and legal risks. Gait recognition and other behavioral traits have applications in security, healthcare, and user interface interactions, with ongoing research aiming to improve their reliability and practical deployment.

Voice recognition is prevalent in many current applications and many users are unaware of how it functions. In Chapter 7, we'll take an in-depth look at voice as a biometric trait, considering contexts, functioning, and risks.

CHAPTER 7

Voice

The unique sound of our voice is shaped by the vibration of our vocal cords and influenced by factors such as speed, frequency, and other physiological and behavioral characteristics. It can serve as a distinct identifier and maybe even an early indication of illnesses.

These unique vocal attributes can provide reliable means for individual identification and authentication. Our voice is always with us and therefore voice recognition is not just a natural but a viable method for verifying personal identity in various applications and interactions with digital devices.

Voice-based biometrics is considered a behavioral trait because many vocal characteristics stem from habitual use rather than just the anatomical structure of the voice-producing organs. This makes our voice a good example of a trait that consists of multiple behavioral features, which are influenced by anatomical characteristics, rather than being defined by them.

While all biometric traits blend physiological and behavioral elements to some extent, the balance of these components can vary. For instance, some voice characteristics are shaped by the physical aspects of the voice box or vocal cords. Whether a biometric system is labeled as behavioral or physiological therefore depends on which features are extracted.

CHAPTER 7   VOICE

What Characteristics Make Voice a Suitable Biometric Trait?

The use of voice to interact with technology has increased significantly in recent years. The spoken word is seen as a natural way to interact with technology as it mimics the communication between people. It can also offer an easier way for people with accessibility challenges like poor eyesight or literacy challenges to interact with digital services. It can also make interaction with devices safer in situations where the user should keep their hands and eyes on something else—for example, when driving, operating heavy machinery, kneading dough, etc.

The human voice also contains a lot of information that can enable the identification and analysis of behavioral and physiological traits. Individuals' voice sounds differ due to the physiological characteristics of their voice organs and the way they speak, such as speed, intervals, variation, etc.

Like other inheritance factors, our voice, which is a basic characteristic, is always with us—with exceptions caused by health conditions. Unlike fingerprints, our voices change over time as we get older. The reason children have higher voices comes from the fact that the voice box (larynx) is smaller. As we go through puberty, the voice box grows and the voice gets deeper.[1]

Another factor that impacts the pitch of our voice is the tightness of the vocal cords as they contract when the air from the lungs hits them. They become less flexible as we age.

The relative stability of our voice over time is certainly a strength of this biometric signal to perform identification based on our voice and also detect changes that can indicate medical or physiological issues.

---

[1] How voice changes as we age www.britannica.com/story/why-does-your-voice-change-as-you-age.

One of the major disadvantages of using the voice for authentication is that it's a biometric trait we leave behind as we use it. When creating digital content—audio or video—our voice becomes part of the public domain and is not a secret trait anymore. We'll go into more detail about how recorded audio can be used to bypass voice-based authentication.

How Voice Is Captured

The process of using voice as a biometric signal begins with a microphone capturing sound vibrations. In simple terms, the microphone converts these vibrations into a continuous electric signal, which is subjected to sophisticated analysis by electronic components. It is then processed for biometric identification.

In the realm of voice biometrics, this process involves more than just recognizing spoken words or phrases like the activation commands used by smart speakers such as "Ok Google," "Hey Siri," or "Alexa." It extends to analyzing the unique characteristics of an individual's voice, which include pitch, tone, rhythm, and distinct speech patterns. By examining these elements, the system can identify subtle nuances that differentiate one person's voice from another.

Strengths and Weaknesses

In the realm of authentication and identification voice biometrics have emerged as a prevalent technology. This section delves into the inherent strengths and weaknesses of using voice as a biometric trait.

CHAPTER 7   VOICE

Strengths

Natural and Intuitive Interaction

Voice interaction with technology is innately more natural than moving a cursor across a screen. It's meant to reflect the way humans communicate. This ease of use has greatly influenced its increasing adoption in technology interfaces. This doesn't mean that the dialogue between human and machine is perfect, but for selected applications, it has reached the level of efficiency that it aims at.

Inherent Personal Trait

Voice is an intrinsic characteristic that is consistently present in individuals, except under certain health conditions. This consistent availability renders it a convenient choice for biometric identification.

Medical and Physiological Insights

Changes in voice over time can offer valuable medical insights. Age and health conditions influence these changes, making voice a useful tool in health monitoring and diagnosis.

Behavioral analysis

Voice contains several features that are behavioral in nature, which allows for contextual signals like sentiments to be extractable.

Technological Accessibility

Voice biometrics only require a microphone, a common component in consumer electronics. Unlike some biometrics that need specialized hardware, this widespread technological availability makes it an accessible option in a variety of devices.

Weaknesses

Public Domain Exposure

Regular use of voice in digital media can lead to its exposure in the public domain, potentially compromising its confidentiality and security in authentication contexts.

Variability and Aging

As individuals get older, physiological factors cause their voices to change. This variability can challenge the consistent accuracy of voice recognition systems over time.

Vulnerability to Digital Misuse

The ease of digitally recording and manipulating voices increases their vulnerability to sophisticated attacks, such as replay and AI-generated impersonations, posing significant security risks.

In What Contexts Are They Used?

Voice used as a biometric trait has benefited multiple sectors, notably in identification and authentication, communication, and healthcare. In identification, it offers a way to verify identities, which is widely used in banking and security systems. In communication, voice assists in enhancing interactions between users and digital devices, exemplified by smart speakers and voice-controlled applications. In healthcare, it's a burgeoning tool for early disease detection and patient monitoring, leveraging unique vocal patterns to identify health issues. This multifaceted utility of voice underscores its growing significance in our technologically driven world.

Smart Speakers and Personal Assistants

Smart speakers and personal assistants represent a significant area where voice is being used as a biometric trait. Since Alexa was introduced by Amazon in 2014, the industry has expanded with numerous other technology providers launching their voice-activated assistants, such as Google Assistant and Apple Siri. These technologies are integrated into Android smartphones, stand-alone smart speakers, and Apple devices, respectively. Manufacturers of home appliances and security systems have also taken advantage of these platforms to enhance their functionality, offering a voice-based interaction for their users. These devices function by constantly listening for specific activation phrases or keywords.

CHAPTER 7 VOICE

Once a keyword like "Hey Siri," "Ok Google," or "Alexa" is detected, the device activates and starts processing further spoken commands. If a user has set up a voice profile, the system can identify the speaker, adding a layer of personalization to the interaction. The assistant then transcribes the spoken words into text, analyzes the query, and responds appropriately. The responses can range from providing information based on publicly available data to accessing personal details like calendar appointments, reminders, or even controlling smart home devices, assuming the appropriate permissions and settings are in place.

Smart speakers are designed to be stationary and are usually placed in a home or office where they have constant access to power and Internet connectivity. This setup allows them to process queries quickly and remain ready for user interaction. The continuous development in this field focuses on enhancing voice recognition accuracy, improving the quality of interactions, and expanding the range of tasks these assistants can perform. This makes them an increasingly integral part of individuals' daily life and routines.

My Voice Is My Password

In banking, the "My Voice is My Password" feature employs voice biometrics for customer identification. When customers set up this feature, they record a specific sentence, creating a voice profile associated with their account. When they interact with the bank afterward, the system prompts them to say a sentence, which can be the one they recorded or another predetermined phrase. The call center software then analyzes the spoken words, focusing on voice characteristics such as tone, pitch, and rhythm. It compares these elements with the customer's stored voice profile to verify their identity. This process aims to ensure that the person calling is indeed the account holder, offering a balance between security and convenience. Such a system represents a practical application of voice biometrics in a real-world scenario, providing an alternative to traditional security methods like PINs or security questions.

Sentiment Analysis

Sentiment analysis through voice biometrics involves interpreting emotions and attitudes from spoken words, a field that has seen significant research and technological investment. This process entails analyzing the content of speech as well as its tonal qualities, pace, volume, and inflections, which can reveal a speaker's emotional state.

In practical applications, such as in customer service, this technology can be used to gauge a customer's mood or level of agitation before a conversation even starts. This enables customer care agents to tailor their approach, potentially improving the interaction's outcome. Similarly, in media analysis, sentiment analysis can be applied to assess the emotional tone of spoken content in videos, providing insights into public reactions or the effectiveness of communication strategies.

However, the effectiveness of sentiment analysis through voice remains a subject of ongoing research, with mixed results. Challenges include accurately interpreting nuances across different languages, dialects, and individual speech patterns. Additionally, the context in which words are spoken plays a crucial role, and separating genuine emotional indicators from sarcasm or irony continues to be a complex task for these systems. Despite these challenges, the potential of voice-based sentiment analysis in enhancing communication and understanding in various domains remains a promising and evolving area of study.

Early Detection of Diseases

The exploration of voice analysis for early disease detection represents a promising frontier in medical research. Recent advancements have focused on how changes in voice patterns can serve as indicators for various health conditions. This approach stems from the understanding that diseases often cause subtle changes in voice qualities, such as alterations in tone, pitch, rhythm, or speech clarity.

For example, research has shown potential in using voice analysis to detect neurological conditions like Parkinson's disease, where vocal changes can be one of the early symptoms. Similarly, respiratory diseases may impact breath control during speech, thereby affecting voice quality. Even mood disorders and mental health conditions might be detectable through changes in speech patterns.

These developments involve sophisticated algorithms and machine-learning techniques that analyze vocal characteristics to identify deviations from an individual's normal speech patterns. The goal is to develop non-invasive, cost-effective methods for early diagnosis, potentially leading to earlier interventions and better health outcomes.

However, it's important to note that this field is still in its nascent stages, and, while promising, voice analysis for disease detection requires further research and validation to become a widely used clinical tool. The challenge lies in ensuring accuracy across diverse populations and accounting for variations in voices due to factors unrelated to health conditions.

Smart Speakers

In this chapter, we're going to dive into the ways smart speakers such as Amazon's Alexa, Google Home devices, and others work. Here's a step-by-step explanation of the journey between someone saying "Alexa" or "Ok google" until they (hopefully) receive the desired response.

1. Detecting human voice: The journey begins with the smart speaker "listening" for human voices, specifically within the range of 85 to 255 Hertz, which is the typical frequency range of human speech. The speaker is on the lookout for an "activation phrase" or "wake word" such as "Hey Alexa," "Hey Google," or "Hey Siri." These phrases signal the speaker to actively start processing further instructions.

2. Activation Phrase Recognition: Upon hearing the sound, the speaker analyzes it to check if it matches the activation phrase. This analysis is done by an internal chip equipped with artificial intelligence, ensuring quick processing while maintaining user privacy by not sending this data to external servers.

3. Speaker Identification: In systems where a voice profile is set up, the speaker compares the voice with stored profiles to recognize the speaker. This step allows the device to provide personalized responses or access to specific user data.

4. Understanding the Request: After recognizing the speaker and the intent to interact, the smart speaker records the subsequent spoken words, which are then transcribed into text and sent to a centralized service (like the cloud) for further analysis to understand the request.

5. Responding to the Request: Finally, the speaker provides a response based on the analyzed request. This could range from answering questions to controlling smart home devices.

It is important to note that different models and brands of smart speakers may have variations in how they process and respond to voice commands. These nuances can be based on the specific technology used by each brand or model.

CHAPTER 7 VOICE

Environmental Factors

Environmental factors significantly impact the collection and processing of voice data in biometric systems. Understanding these factors is crucial for the effective design and implementation of voice recognition technology.

　　Background Noise: Ambient noise is a major factor affecting voice recognition. In noisy environments such as crowded areas or locations with heavy machinery, distinguishing the speaker's voice from background noise becomes challenging, reducing recognition accuracy. While advanced systems employ noise cancellation techniques, completely eliminating this interference remains a complex issue.

- Acoustic Conditions: Acoustics, such as echoes in large halls or sound absorption in carpeted rooms, can significantly affect voice capture. These conditions can alter how a voice is perceived by microphones, leading to potential errors in voice recognition.

- Distance from Microphone: The effectiveness of voice recognition is also influenced by the distance between the speaker and the microphone. Greater distances can result in the microphone not capturing the voice clearly, decreasing accuracy. Optimal performance is often achieved when the user is within a specific range of the device.

- Presence of Multiple Voices: In settings where several people are speaking simultaneously, voice recognition systems may struggle to isolate individual voices. This issue is particularly prevalent in public or communal spaces.

- Voice Variations Due to Health: Health conditions, such as colds, sore throats, or allergies, can temporarily alter a person's voice. These changes can affect the tone, pitch, and clarity of the voice, posing a challenge for the system to accurately match the voice with its stored profile.

To ensure their reliability and accuracy in real-world conditions, each of these environmental factors must be carefully considered in the development of voice biometric systems.

How Does the Aging Voice Impact Its Use as a Biometric Signal?

Voice biometrics is distinct from other biometric traits in several ways, particularly in how it travels through space and can penetrate materials like walls. Unlike biometrics that require close proximity or direct line of sight, such as fingerprint or iris recognition, voice biometrics can be effective over a distance and does not require visual contact. Voice recognition systems validate an individual's identity by analyzing specific characteristics of their voice, focusing on vocal features rather than the sound or pronunciation of speech.

Automated voice recognition systems can accurately identify individuals by their voices with less than a 1% error rate, comparable to the accuracy of fingerprint systems. This accuracy is even higher when speakers use a pre-determined phrase. However, voice-based systems usually require cooperation from the subject and are affected by factors like noisy environments, the emotional condition of the user, and health conditions, which can change the voice and impact recognition.

CHAPTER 7   VOICE

Voice biometrics' ability to operate effectively over a distance and through barriers sets it apart from other biometric methods, offering unique advantages in various applications. It does, however, also face challenges such as being influenced by external environmental factors and the physical and emotional state of the user.

Risks and Attack Methods

Just like any other biometric trait, voice can be at risk of being used for bad actors to compromise other people's accounts and impersonate them:

- Replay Attacks: A common risk in voice recognition is the "replay attack." Imagine someone recording your voice and then playing it back to trick a system into thinking it is you. This kind of deception is surprisingly simple to do with a basic recorder and playback device. In more advanced cases, a scammer might even prompt someone to say certain phrases over a call and then use those recordings for malicious purposes.

- AI-Generated Voice Impersonation: Another growing concern is the use of artificial intelligence (AI) to mimic voices. Modern AI can analyze a person's voice characteristics, like how high or low it is and how fast they speak, to create a very convincing fake voice. This technology can be misused to impersonate people for fraudulent activities, especially if the AI has access to enough samples of the targeted person's voice.

Preventing Misuse

To combat these risks, voice recognition systems are becoming smarter by the day. They can now check for "liveness"—clues that indicate whether a voice is live or recorded. For example, they might listen for background

CHAPTER 7   VOICE

sounds that match throughout a conversation, helping to confirm the speaker is real and present. Moreover, some systems may ask users to say something unexpected or a phrase that changes every time, making it hard for imposters with pre-recorded clips to succeed. These measures continuously evolve to enhance security and ensure the person speaking is in fact who they claim to be.

Summary

Using voice to interact with technology is a natural evolution. While created by a combination of structural features and habitual use, voice is considered a behavioral biometric trait. In Chapter 7, we have considered the strengths and weaknesses, contexts in which it is used as well as considerations which are unique to voice analysis.

Chapter 7 rounds out Part 2, in which we had a look at Face, Voice, and various other physiological and behavioral traits. In Part 3, we take a broader view of biometric data as a field by looking at how well it functions in real-world contexts. In Chapter 8, we think critically about accuracy and what it means in the context of biometric data use.

PART III

Critical Analysis

CHAPTER 8

How Do We Judge Accuracy?

Now that we've looked at what the field of Biometrics is and taken a closer look at several specific sources of biometric data, we're going to step back and define some of the ways we talk about performance in terms of correctness. We'll think critically about what it means to be correct and we'll consider the various factors contributing to the effectiveness of biometrics.

What Does It Mean to Be Correct?

There are a variety of ways to think about correctness. But what does it mean to say something is right, or correct? A simple statement of fact can be true or false, right or wrong. A more complex statement can have degrees of correctness. Can be partially correct, or possibly be considered close enough. We could spend considerable time discussing logic circuits to discover that a statement must be entirely true to be considered logically true.

But many times, we are not dealing in the arena of restating known facts or determining the conclusion of a set of logically sound statements. We may be taking a measurement of a real-world item or substance and then making a decision based on that measurement. Measurements are never perfect. In real situations of taking measurements and drawing conclusions, there are many points at which the correctness of the final result can be compromised.

CHAPTER 8   HOW DO WE JUDGE ACCURACY?

In this section, we'll define the following terms, all of which help us talk about different aspects of correctness:

- Accuracy
- Precision
  - Of a measurement
  - Of a measuring device
- Validity
- Reliability (Consistency)
  - Of a signal or trait being measured
  - Of a device or measuring tool
- Robustness

An important detail to keep in mind when discussing the correctness of measurements is that we usually don't have the correct value to compare it to. In the real world, we're usually measuring something because we don't know how much it measures. Our best estimate of the true value is the one we have just found—by measuring.

What is preferable, being accurate or being precise? To say a device measures with a high level of accuracy—is that the same as saying it measures to a high degree of precision? Unless a person has had reason to consider the difference between these two concepts, there is a good chance they may believe accuracy and precision are essentially the same. They aren't.

Accuracy—*Accuracy* is a measure of how close a value is to the correct one. A tool can be considered accurate if the results it gives are within an acceptable tolerance of the true measure.

Precision—*Precision* can be thought of in two ways. The precision of a measurement can be a reference to the size of the units to which it has been measured. A length measured to the nearest millimeter is more precise than the same length measured to the nearest centimeter.

A device or method of measurement can be considered *precise* if it returns multiple measurements of the same item that are very close to one another.

While accuracy and precision can describe the correctness of a measurement, Validity and Reliability can be used to describe the correctness of a test.

Validity—Is the result of the test or analysis legitimate? Analogous to accuracy, validity describes the degree to which a test actually measures what it is supposed to. A test is valid if it measures what it was intended to measure.

Reliability—Just like a scale that consistently returns very similar values can be called precise, a test or analytical process can be considered reliable if it consistently returns results that are grouped very closely together. In the context of biometrics, reliability can refer to the device which measures and analyzes the biometric signal, or it can refer to the signal itself.

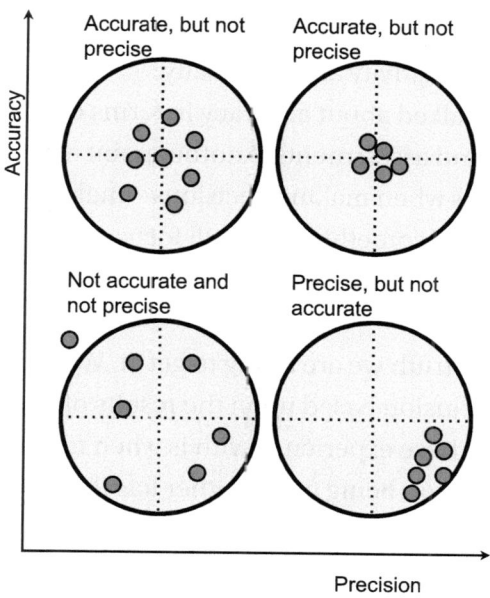

Figure 8-1. *Visuallizing accuracy and precision*

CHAPTER 8   HOW DO WE JUDGE ACCURACY?

In Figure 8-1, we see Accuracy and Validity can be represented by points clustered around the correct answer or result, though not necessarily close to one another. Precision or reliability can be represented by points clustered close to one another, though not necessarily around the correct answer. It's easy to conclude that the goal would be to have tightly clustered points, centered around the correct answer.

Robustness—Robustness describes how resistant a test or procedure is to destabilizing forces. In statistical analysis, this could mean not all the required hypotheses are satisfied; in biometrics, it could mean an environmental factor is reducing the quality of the biometric data received for processing.

What Is an Error?

There are many ways to be wrong. If we take all the terms we just discussed in the last section, a lack of any of those qualities can produce a version of incorrectness. In this section, we will add two terms to the list begun in the previous section—sensitivity and specificity.

So far we have talked about accuracy in terms of measurements and collection of data and assessments. Another point at which we should consider accuracy is when making decisions—making a judgment about the state or veracity of something. We will focus on situations in which a measurement is taken and processed, and then a decision of yes or no is made.

Often, there is a truth we are trying to get at. We perform an analysis and come to a conclusion based upon the results of our analysis. A version of this most people have experience with is when testing for a disease. Let's assume the person being tested either has the disease or they don't. There's no middle ground. And the test performed returns either a positive or a negative result.

It soon becomes clear that there are four cases in a situation like this—these four possible outcomes are illustrated in Figure 8-2. A person infected with the disease could test positive or negative; and a person free of this disease could test positive or negative. As we see from the following chart, two of the four cases produce a correct or true result, while the other two cases produce false results. In the case of an infected person testing negative, we call this a *false negative*. Where a person free of the disease gets a positive result, this is called a *false positive*.

	Infected	Free of Infection
Tests +	Correct Result	**False Positive**
Tests -	**False Negative**	Correct Result

Figure 8-2.

Tests such as pregnancy tests and covid tests that have been put through a rigorous quality control process will have published accuracy rates. But it is essential that we see there are two different ways the test must be accurate. A test must have good results in both detecting which subjects actually have the condition being tested for, while also correctly determining when a subject does not have the condition being tested for.

Sensitivity

How reliably a test detects the condition being tested for is called *sensitivity*. How sensitive the test is tells us how well it can catch cases of the condition it is looking for. A sensitivity of 99% would tell us that, assuming the test is performed correctly under appropriate conditions, 99% of cases presenting with the condition of interest will be detected by the test. While a test can never actually have 100% sensitivity, getting as close as possible within the constraints of budget and practicality is usually the goal.

CHAPTER 8   HOW DO WE JUDGE ACCURACY?

Specificity

Of course, a test must also reliably return negative results for subjects not having the condition being tested for. The percentage of times a test will return a negative result for a subject not having the condition is called *specificity*.

A way of keeping sensitivity separate from specificity is to see the subjects being tested as two distinct populations. Sensitivity addresses how well the test reports on the population that does have the condition. A high sensitivity catches a larger percentage of this population and correctly assigns them a positive result.

Specificity addresses how well the test reports on the population that does not have the condition. A high specificity assigns a larger percentage of this population a correct negative result.

Type I and Type II Errors

What happens when the test is wrong? A test with 99% sensitivity will miss 1% of positive cases and incorrectly assign them a negative designation. If the same test has 98% specificity, then 2% of the population without the condition will be falsely given a positive result. Figure 8-3 expands on the ideas from Figure 8-2.

	Population with condition Test has 99% Sensitivity	Population free of condition Test has 98% Specificity
Tests +	Correct Result 99% of relevant population	False Positive 2% of relevant population
Tests -	False Negative 1% of relevant population	Correct Result 98% of relevant population

Figure 8-3.

CHAPTER 8   HOW DO WE JUDGE ACCURACY?

Let's imagine a scenario in which a patient tests positive for a disease that is always fatal within a week of diagnosis. The test has 99% sensitivity and 98% specificity. The doctor giving the news of the positive test, instead of suggesting the patient start making final arrangements, smiles and says not to be too worried, "there's less than 10% chance you really have the dreaded illness. Let's retest."

What? Why! Something *must* be wrong!

Not necessarily. Here's how that could happen. If the condition is rare, in this example if it occurs in only 0.2% (1 in 500) of the population, the numbers could work out as stated earlier.

Let's think this through using a population of 100,000, of which 0.2% (200 people) have the dreaded disease.

	Has the Disease	Free from the Disease	Row totals
Tests +	Correct Result 198 99% of relevant population	False Positive 1,996 2% of relevant population	2194
Tests -	False Negative 2 1% of relevant population	Correct Result 97,804 95% of relevant population	97,806
Column totals	200	99,800	100,000

There's a lot to parse through in this table. Firstly, we can see that just over 98% of people tested will get a correct result (97,804+198 = 98,002). So how can this patient be told their diagnosis is not even 10% likely to be true?

In order to fully understand the scenario, we have to go back to thinking about populations. The chart is divided into populations (columns) based on who has the disease and who does not. But the person being tested doesn't know which of these two populations they fall into.

That's the whole reason they took the test. Once this person receives their positive result, the only population they know they belong to is the population of people with a positive test result. We can see in the last column that this population consists of 2,194 people. Of these 2,194, only 198 (or less than 9%) actually have the disease. The disproportionately high number of people without the disease means the low percentage of false positives translates into a number significantly high than correct positive results.

Aside from the shock a patient may suffer when told they are pregnant, or have covid, we might wonder what's the harm in a false positive if we can retest? In practice, the risk of false positives can be reduced in several ways, one of which being that we only test for a condition if we have reasonable suspicion the condition is present. Statistically, the way to prevent false positives would be to increase the specificity of the test. Of course, this would increase the cost of developing and possibly producing the test.

The same goes for false negatives. One would be justified in arguing that, where a disease is involved, a false negative would have a more profound impact. Again, increasing sensitivity would decrease the occurrence of false negative, but at what cost? At some point, good enough has to be good enough. Developers of medical tests, and biometric sensors, have to make decisions based on cost, speed, size of the device, and impact of both types of mistakes to settle on a level of error that will be acceptable.

Performance of Various Methods

We have looked at several sources of biometric data and considered a variety of problems we can solve with biometrics. Now we look at how we can think about the performance of biometrics in various contexts.

The Layers of Quality

Using biometric data to solve problems of identity is a multistage process. Each stage introduces new potential for error. Firstly, the source of the biometric information might be corrupted. A windy day could impact the capture of a voice recording, greasy hands could prevent a clean fingerprint being taken. Biometrics "left behind" like fingerprints at a crime scene have lower quality than a deliberately provided fingerprint on a fingerprint scanner in optimal conditions. Secondly, the detection of the biometric information—the quality or condition of the sensor—could be a source of error. Camera resolution and noise-filtering capabilities of the microphone are some specifications that can influence the quality of the raw biometric data being collected. Thirdly, the analysis of the biometric information—the algorithm or procedure used—might have a flaw, or lack robustness, or simply be inefficient. At each of these three points along the way, the process is at risk.

The Difficulty of Comparing Biometrics

As Biometrics are used in a broad set of situations and there are various types of biometric signals, the question around performance is rarely as straightforward as coming up with a single value. In this part of the chapter, we're looking at a few dimensions on how the performance of biometrics can be assessed and how the most common types of biometric signals perform. The individual performance also highly depends on the specific implementation.

While discussing their performance, we won't attempt to rank different types of biometric signals or methods in order to determine "which ones are the best." There are many factors that positively or negatively impact the ability to successfully analyze a set of biometric information, and there is not an orderly way to rank the various methods.

CHAPTER 8   HOW DO WE JUDGE ACCURACY?

When discussing the performance of different uses of biometric data, we'll focus on the following indicators:

Performance indicator	Description
Accuracy	The level to which the system correctly identifies a set of biometric information
Robustness	How much environmental factors such as light, noise, temperature, movement, etc. impact the accuracy of the process
Speed	How quickly a system can receive, recognize, and analyze a set of biometric information
Security	How hard it is to spoof the biometric information

Fingerprint

The use of fingerprints to identify someone can have an accuracy of 95–99%. This range depends greatly on the circumstances. Accuracy levels are often used to describe the likelihood of two fingerprints being mistaken for each other. Apple states that, using even a small area of the fingerprint, the risk of making this error is 1 in 50,000.[1]

While popular culture might lead us to believe fingerprint evidence is indisputable, false positives in forensics occur at a rate of about 0.1%.[2] At border control, accuracy levels of fingerprint matching have been recorded up to 99.9%.[3]

---

[1] Fingerprint accuracy https://support.apple.com/en-us/HT204587.
[2] False Positive forensic https://blogs.ubc.ca/communicatingchem2019w209/2019/03/20/fingerprint/#:~:text=In%20one%20study%2C%20researchers%20found,forensic%20experts%20perceive%20the%20evidence.
[3] Border control www.nist.gov/news-events/news/2004/07/nist-study-shows-computerized-fingerprint-matching-highly-accurate.

The robustness of this method can be impacted by factors impacting the sensors such as wear on the plate, moisture, and extreme temperatures. Also, while the pattern remains constant throughout life, certain exposures can reduce the appearance of fingerprints. With age, skin becomes less elastic, thickening the ridges in fingerprints.[4] This can make it more difficult to achieve an accurate read.

As a mode of identifying people, fingerprint analysis is fast with high security. The speed depends mainly upon the software used to match reference points, while the high degree of security is due to the uniqueness of fingerprints from person to person. The difficulty and cost in producing a replica fingerprint varies greatly based on the method used, but it is always a one-off effort, thus making it expensive for the attacker.

Voice Recognition

Voice recognition has a medium to high accuracy. The performance of this method greatly depends on the size of the dataset the sample voice is being compared to. Identifying the correct person from a small group like a family, as with home devices, tends to be more accurate than from a set of millions of people.

Voice recognition has a medium level of robustness. Many factors can cause the quality of a voice recording to vary. A few examples of this might be the distance of the person from the microphone, the quality of the microphone, the noise level around the person speaking, the diction used when speaking. All of these can have an impact on the quality of the results.

Compared with fingerprint analysis, Voice recognition has medium speed and security. The bottleneck with speed is the time it takes the person to speak the words required for the system to analyze their content and origin. While our voice has a lot of unique characteristics that allow

---

[4] www.sciencefocus.com/the-human-body/can-fingerprints-change-during-a-lifetime/.

it to be distinguished from different people, it also is easy to be recorded and replayed. Because the speaker doesn't have to be physically present to provide their voice-based biometrics, liveness is more difficult to assess and replay attacks are easier to perform. Numerous new technologies exist in the space of Generative AI (Artificial Intelligence) that allow attackers to replicate other people's voices based on pre-recorded content. This is much more a problem for targeted attacks, thus creating a high cost of attack.

Facial Recognition

According to the NIST Facial Recognition Vendor test, accuracy levels up to 99.7% can be achieved in ideal circumstances.[5] In less ideal situations like pictures "captured in the wild," error rates would climb up to 9.3%.

Light, positioning, and image quality can all negatively influence the information available for face recognition, when performed with a 2D image alone. Aging can also negatively impact the effectiveness of facial recognition. The NIST test showed the error rate with a picture taken 18 years prior increasing up to tenfold.

Of the three methods presented in this section, Facial recognition can be the slowest process. The time it takes to take a picture in an ideal situation (light, position) like a mug shot or a proper passport picture can be minutes. The security can vary greatly depending on the original setup. When performing facial recognition based on a 2D image taken by a camera (webcam, smartphone camera), replay attacks or impersonations are more successful than if additional sensors like infrared mapping are added.

---

[5] NIST Face www.csis.org/blogs/strategic-technologies-blog/how-accurate-are-facial-recognition-systems-and-why-does-it#:~:text=In%20ideal%20conditions%2C%20facial%20recognition,Recognition%20Vendor%20Test%20(FRVT).

Summary

In this chapter, we've taken a more theoretical look at the concept of being correct. Accuracy and precision, along with their analogous concepts of validity and reliability, work together to form a complete concept of correctness. Sensitivity and specificity also work together in creating a test that optimizes sensitivity and specificity.

This way of understanding correctness and errors is then applied to assess the performance of various uses of biometric data.

Having thought about the accuracy of the results of a biometric system, we move on to Chapter 9, where we consider the risks and responsibilities involved in using biometric data.

CHAPTER 9

Challenges and Responsibilities

Did you know? Algorithms analyzing biometric information can have lower accuracy for people of color. This can lead to higher hurdles for some people to access services, where biometric identification or authentication is required.

When we look at the progress technology has made in this space, it's easy to be impressed by the opportunities that we now have—opportunities that were pure science fiction merely a decade ago. In this chapter, we address some of the challenges and responsibilities when using biometric signals. While some are generic, others are more specific to their application.

We introduce some of the bigger topics such as data privacy laws, why classifiers show bias, and the broader legal implications—leaving deeper discussions for other forums.

CHAPTER 9 CHALLENGES AND RESPONSIBILITIES

Matching of Biometrics Is Probabilistic in Nature

Biometric systems, which rely on the matching and analysis of physiological and behavioral traits, inherently lack perfect accuracy and are probabilistic by nature. The process of collecting biometric data—whether it involves highly distinctive features such as fingerprints or iris patterns—is susceptible to variations. Repeated measurements of the same trait won't yield identical results.

Factors such as the pressure applied when scanning a fingerprint, the angle of interaction, the dryness of the skin, and other environmental conditions at the time of data capture all introduce inconsistencies in the measurement process. The same is true for other biometric traits.

When using biometric information to assess someone's identity, level of activity, or state of well-being, the measurement comes with a degree of uncertainty. Conclusions can only be made with a certain degree of confidence, rather than absolute certainty.

Consequences of Errors

When building resilience for systems that rely on biometric signals, we must recognize the potential for mistakes. In this section, we provide you with a mental model for anticipating the potential consequences of biometric data inaccuracies.

There's a diverse list of consequences that can be caused by the erroneous use of biometrics. They can be far-reaching and require us to ask critical questions to predict the gravity of these outcomes:

- **Monetary Impact:** Using biometric traits for identification and authentication comes with a risk of false-acceptance rates. This can be malicious attackers attempting to trick the system by impersonating a legitimate person to gain access to someone else's bank accounts or cryptocurrency wallets.

- **Harm to Individuals:** Matching biometric information with existing databases is a commonly used practice in law enforcement when looking for suspects. False positives in matching images gathered from surveillance cameras can lead to the wrong person being arrested.

- **Privacy Breaches:** Biometric data in itself is sensitive and personal, but it often also is meant to protect access to private information. A breach could result in private information falling into the hands of unauthorized individuals, be they malicious actors with the intent to exploit this data or accidental recipients with no ill intent.

- **Legal Repercussions:** In the context of law enforcement or judicial proceedings, there are consequences if an innocent individual is wrongfully implicated due to a biometric mismatch.

- **Accountability:** The reliability of a company's biometric system is intimately tied to its public image and operational integrity. A single biometric error could lead to a loss of user trust, negative publicity, and legal challenges, ultimately affecting the company's bottom line and its capacity to conduct business.

Understanding these types of consequences, of which there are certainly more, helps us determine the potential harm that could result from the erroneous use of biometrics.

Identify the Risk of Getting It Wrong

No two instances of biometric measurements, even from the same individual, are exactly the same. There are several methods of assessing risks and predicting potential outcomes from decisions made based on biometric measurements. These methods are also useful in contexts other than biometrics worth understanding in the context of this topic. In this chapter, we provide a summary of these methods which will serve as initial guidance on how to think about assessing risks when using biometrics:

Failure Modes and Effects Analysis (FMEA)

FMEA is a systematic, step-by-step approach for identifying all possible failures in a design, manufacturing, or assembly process, or a product or service. It's used to assess the impact of each failure and prioritize the actions that should be taken to mitigate the associated risks and prevent them from occurring.

Decision Analysis/Decision Trees

Decision analysis, often visualized through decision trees, is a quantitative method that's used to make informed choices by structuring and analyzing decisions based on different risks, outcomes, and the impact of various options, often through a graphical representation of alternatives.

Statistical Significance and Confidence Intervals

These are fundamental concepts in statistics that assess the reliability of an estimate. Statistical significance tests whether an observed effect is likely due to chance, while confidence intervals provide a range within which we can expect the true value to lie.

Monte Carlo Simulations

Monte Carlo simulations are used to model the probability of different outcomes in processes that are inherently unpredictable, to calculate the associated risks. They do so by running multiple trial runs, or simulations, using random variables.

Scenario Planning

Scenario planning is a strategic method that allows organizations to explore and prepare for several possible future environments by developing coherent and plausible scenarios, each detailed enough to allow decision-makers to consider different pathways that might unfold and impact the future of the organization.

Are Biometrics the End of Privacy?

Privacy *A state in which one is not observed or disturbed by other people – Oxford English Dictionary.*

Biometrics technology, which allows the collection and processing of fingerprints, faces, iris, voices, and other human characteristics, has become a common method for authentication and identification. These methods are significantly harder to bypass than traditional methods of authentication like passwords and can be seen as a positive contribution to help individuals and organizations safeguard their private information to deter hackers.

At the same time, the collection and use of biometrics raise important privacy concerns, and while it might not be the end of privacy altogether, it certainly challenges the traditional boundaries and expectations of privacy.

The integration of biometric data processing is increasingly blurring the lines between our digital presence and our physical identity. Initially, the Internet was a realm of forums and semi-anonymous interactions, built without a robust mechanism for authenticating real-world identities. Today, attempts to ensure authenticity often retrofit older technologies to connect with a user's real-world identity.

Biometrics offer a fundamental shift, challenging traditional notions of privacy within this interconnected space. Privacy itself is a complex concept. It's defined by the Oxford English Dictionary as a state free from unwelcome observation or disturbance by others, and by the International Association of Privacy Professionals (IAPP) as the right to solitude or freedom from intrusion. Privacy's definition is as nuanced as its implications.

Our discussion doesn't exhaustively cover the vast scope of privacy but provides illustrative examples and talking points. These insights frame the use of biometric data within the larger privacy debate, recognizing the transformative impact of such technologies on our conception of personal space and identity in the digital age.

It Depends

The short and unsatisfactory answer to whether biometrics are the end of privacy is "it depends." On the one hand, the use of biometrics as a strong authentication method—which is, in most ways, superior to knowledge factors like passwords—makes it harder for unauthorized people to access personal information. Losing exclusive access to a personal email account or system containing personal health records puts the privacy or safety of an individual at risk.

On the other hand, the use of biometric information binds digital information to real-world identities and characteristics. A breach or adversarial use of said information, or the link to seemingly anonymized data, risks individuals' privacy.

These core questions indicate the impact on privacy and the use of biometrics (can) have:

- What type of biometrics is being used?
- What conclusion is being drawn from the use of these biometrics?
- Where is the biometric information processed and stored?
- Who has access to the biometric information?
- What type of identity is the biometric trait linked to, or what can it be linked to?

Common Concerns About Privacy

In recent years, conversations about how new technologies impact people's rights to privacy have increased. Privacy has become integral for business leaders, politicians, and legal experts. It's an understatement to say that it has emerged from just being an afterthought.

Surveillance

Surveillance is an umbrella term for many risks pointed out that are amplified by the use of biometric technology.

Definition of surveillance (Oxford English Dictionary): *close observation, especially of a suspected spy or criminal.*

If we substitute "suspected spy or criminal" with an entity, business, individual, or government organization, the term becomes even harder to grasp. What is surveillance, and what is a legitimate exchange of information? This question has to be looked at from a legal and ethical perspective. Both elements are volatile and diverse spectrums influenced by the (local) circumstances and zeitgeist.

The main point comes back to the connection between digital and real-world identities that are now always desired by the user and, in some cases, abused by actors with ill intent.

Situational Compartmentalization

Our privacy doesn't only rely on our ability to keep certain information secret, but also on the natural compartmentalization in which the information is being created in our lives. While my face might end up in a picture, when attending a demonstration with thousands of other people, I tend to rely on this data not being connected with the time I entered into a bank to withdraw money from my bank account or apply for a job.

While I can't reasonably expect that my presence in either location will not be documented in any digital form, it's still a valid expectation that these occurrences are separated from each other. Less by relying on legal or regulatory guidelines, but more because of the compartmentalized nature of said data.

The moment this compartmentalization breaks down, the concept of privacy is put into question.

The example of search engines for faces using facial recognition earlier in the book is a timely way to describe how situational compartmentalization can be broken. What used to be reasonable expectations, regarding how pictures of ourselves separate from our identity, might no longer be valid in the future.

CHAPTER 9   CHALLENGES AND RESPONSIBILITIES

Racial Bias in Biometrics

The potential for racial bias in biometric technology has raised concerns about profiling and discrimination. This technology, utilized by both consumers and law enforcement, has faced intense scrutiny for potentially exacerbating inequalities. Privacy and civil liberties organizations have pointed out that the technology's inaccuracies disproportionately affect groups whose rights are often marginalized, with studies indicating that facial recognition systems tend to be most accurate with white male faces. For instance, the accuracy rates for people of color and women are markedly lower compared to the near 99% rates observed for white males.

Racial bias can lead to exclusion from common services and disproportionate scrutiny in other areas:

Exclusion from common services	Failure to pass face-based identity verifications, can make it harder to get access to financial services
Disproportionate scrutiny	Increased false-positives in law enforcement can cause innocent people being put under scrutiny.

The "Gender Shades[1]" research project has analyzed some of the more widely used algorithms for facial recognition. Their research involving 1,270 individuals from six countries—three European and three African—revealed that AI-powered gender recognition algorithms were least accurate with darker-skinned female faces, with disparities ranging from 20% to 34% in accuracy. Such findings underscore the ongoing challenges of racial and gender bias in facial recognition technology.

---

[1] Gender Shades Research program—http://gendershades.org/overview.html.

CHAPTER 9 CHALLENGES AND RESPONSIBILITIES

Gender classifier	Lighter male	Darker male	Darker female	Lighter female	Largest gap
a	100%	94.0%	79.2%	98.3%	20.8%
b	99.2%	99.3%	65.5%	94.0%	33.8%
c	99.7%	88.0%	65.3%	92.9%	34.4%

Different facial recognition systems show significantly less racial bias due to variations in implementation and algorithm design. Despite these advancements, the issue remains contentious. The industry and academic sector continue to grapple with these biases, even as new technologies—some using flawed training data and algorithms—are rolled out regularly.

It's Not Just the Technology

Civil liberty groups, like the ACLU of Minnesota,[2] have raised alarms over the disparities in facial recognition accuracy across different skin tones and genders, viewing it as a continuation of historical and systemic discrimination. Such concerns are grounded in past practices, like the "lantern laws" of the 18th century, which mandated that black people carry a lantern after dark, ostensibly to keep their faces visible.

This legacy of discrimination finds parallels in modern initiatives like Detroit's Project Green Light,[3] launched in 2016. This network of high-definition cameras, providing live feeds to the Detroit Police Department, enables facial recognition against criminal databases and state-issued IDs, effectively putting the state of Michigan's nearly 10 million residents

---

[2] ACLU MN—Article on bias in biometric technology www.aclu-mn.org/en/news/biased-technology-automated-discrimination-facial-recognition.
[3] Project Green Light in Detroit—https://detroitmi.gov/departments/police-department/project-green-light-detroit.

within reach of identification. According to research[4] published by Harvard University, the camera network is more concentrated in predominantly black neighborhoods, while areas with majority white and Asian populations are less targeted.

Critics of the project argue that this uneven deployment perpetuates a longstanding pattern of targeted surveillance and policing in black communities, reflecting a troubling trend of racial bias in law enforcement practices.

Lack of Diversity in Training Data

Accurate facial recognition relies on the breadth and quality of training data used in machine learning algorithms. Within the industry and among privacy advocates, there is an ongoing debate regarding the sufficiency and representativeness of the training data. Some suggest developers may compromise on these aspects to cut costs and accelerate time to market.

One issue is the lack of binding requirements on how training data for classifiers has to be assembled.

Without taking a stance in this debate, it's important to shed light on the challenges of sourcing diverse training data to mitigate discrimination in facial recognition technologies.

Training data is essentially a large collection of facial images that machine learning algorithms use to recognize and verify faces against a stored biometric template. The effectiveness of facial recognition algorithms in real-world applications is directly influenced by the quality, diversity, and volume of this training data. Gathering a vast and representative dataset, with accurately labeled images for algorithm training, is a complex and resource-intensive task.

---

[4] Harvard Research on Bias https://sitn.hms.harvard.edu/flash/2020/racial-discrimination-in-face-recognition-technology/.

There are datasets available to train facial recognition algorithms. Examples like the MS-Celeb-1M,[5] or IMDB-Wiki[6] contain labeled images of people in the public domain, to some extent celebrities. Although many of these widely available datasets are limited for research purposes only and can't be used for commercial applications.

Consent to Collect Biometric Data for Training Purposes

Collecting a vast array of facial images for training facial recognition algorithms presents substantial privacy and consent challenges. Under current privacy laws like the General Data Protection Regulation (GDPR) in the European Union, personal data (including names, addresses, and images) can only be processed with explicit consent. This consent must be freely given for specific purposes, with full disclosure and the option for withdrawal at any time.

Consent is a cornerstone of lawful data processing, particularly for sensitive data like biometrics. National information officers like the ICO[7] in the UK publish information on how the use of biometrics is considered personal information within regulations, in this case GDPR.

Beyond these regulations, there's a growing public reluctance to share biometric data. This wariness is fueled by heightened privacy concerns and the prevalence of data breaches, reinforcing the resistance to consent to broad usage rights.

---

[5] MS-Celeb-1M—https://exposing.ai/msceleb/.
[6] IMDB-Wiki dataset https://data.vision.ee.ethz.ch/cvl/rrothe/imdb-wiki/.
[7] ICO biometrics https://ico.org.uk/for-organisations/uk-gdpr-guidance-and-resources/lawful-basis/biometric-data-guidance-biometric-recognition/how-do-we-process-biometric-data-lawfully/.

CHAPTER 9   CHALLENGES AND RESPONSIBILITIES

Accessibility

Accessibility, often abbreviated as "a11y," is essential in ensuring digital products are usable by people with disabilities. This encompasses a range of abilities, addressing limitations not only in eyesight and hearing but also in movement and cognitive functions. Digital interfaces, like applications and websites, should incorporate functionalities that allow people with disabilities to engage effectively. This includes not just adaptations for those with visual or auditory impairments but also for users with motor difficulties or cognitive constraints.

Examples for assistive features to support people with accessibility needs to use technology:

- **Screenreaders** translate the visible elements of a screen to an audible description. This not only includes text but also interaction elements like buttons, forms, etc.

- **Contrast** can have an impact on how well images and text can be read by people with visual impairments.

The Web Content Accessibility Guidelines (WCAG) are a set of recommendations that guide developers in creating software and hardware that meet these diverse a11y needs. Compliance with a11y is mandated by anti-discrimination laws and employment regulations in many countries, making it a legal and ethical obligation, and it also broadens the usability of biometric systems.

In the realm of biometric systems, inclusive design is critical. For instance, fingerprint scanners should be accessible to individuals in wheelchairs, perhaps through adjustable mounts or alternative positioning, and facial recognition systems need to be sensitive to users who cannot maintain a neutral facial expression due to medical conditions. Moreover, biometric systems should offer alternative authentication options to ensure that all users, regardless of their abilities, have equivalent access to security and identification services.

CHAPTER 9   CHALLENGES AND RESPONSIBILITIES

When it comes to the use of biometrics, accessibility challenges can be broad and subtle. It can be harder for people with muscular or nerve issues that lead to a relevant tremble of their hand to hold their phone still enough to pass a facial authentication step. Such challenges are not "just" an inconvenience but can lead to issues like getting locked out of bank accounts.[8]

The FIDO Alliance, an industry-leading standardization body, has released a white paper[9] in which it describes best practices on how to make authentication methods more accessible.

There are also community-driven resources like the a11yproject.com that provide guidelines and best practices on how to navigate this field and ensure people with all types of abilities are able to use technology without discrimination.

Risks of Collecting and Storing Data

Beyond the legal and regulatory risks that need to be considered when collecting and storing biometric information, we need to understand the practical risks.

The collection and storage of biometric information carry inherent risks that are uniquely challenging compared to traditional security measures like passwords. Unlike passwords, biometric traits are immutable; once compromised, they cannot be changed like a password reset, highlighting the critical issue of irreversibility. This permanence raises significant privacy concerns, as biometric data can reveal highly

---

[8] Hand tremble leads to account lockout (NATWEST) https://info.webusability.co.uk/blog/biometrics-and-natwest-an-accessibility-challenge.

[9] FIDO Alliance a11y best practice https://fidoalliance.org/white-paper-guidance-for-making-fido-deployments-accessible-to-users-with-disabilities/.

personal information. Furthermore, data breaches involving biometric databases can lead to irreversible privacy harm. If fallen into the wrong hands, biometric information can be used for a variety of fraudulent activities that can lead to financial or other harm. A bad actor that gained access to biometric information can use this to connect multiple disconnected, and potentially anonymized identities together, or attempt to bypass protections to access private data.

There is also the risk of potential misuse by authorities, where such data could be used for unwarranted surveillance or other invasive practices. Data storage and retention amplify these risks, as the longer and more widely such data is held, the greater the chance of unauthorized access. Additionally, the technology underpinning biometric systems can sometimes exhibit racial bias, leading to profiling and discrimination. These risks necessitate robust safeguards and transparent policies to protect individuals from misuse and to ensure their privacy and rights are upheld.

Responsibilities

There are several areas in which everyone building solutions using biometrics has to be responsible for potential negative consequences:

- Gathering informed consent and providing transparency
- Prioritizing data security and privacy
- Ensuring accuracy
- Limiting to ethically defensible use
- Compliance and legal considerations

While all of these responsibilities seem to be clear, it's always a good option to include an external council to ensure that a neutral person, without a particular interest in the project, has looked at these aspects when a project involves biometric information.

Gather Informed Consent and Provide Transparency

The focus on consent and transparency has been put at the center of the privacy conversation, especially with data regulations such as GDPR (General Data Protection Regulation) in the EU and similar frameworks.

Data handlers must make it clear to the users what biometric information they use and why they need to collect it. Depending on the type of service they offer, they should ensure that they have adequate alternatives if the user feels uncomfortable providing their biometric information.

In some situations—for example, when employees are being asked to use their biometrics to access company information—the question of options has to be discussed. The UK's Information Commissioner Office (ICO) has concluded[10] that a company that wanted to roll out biometric identification mechanisms, using fingerprints, benefited from a power imbalance. It said that the imbalance between employer and employee would compromise the right to choose, which is embedded in European data regulations.

Prioritize Data Security and Privacy

Robust encryption and protection measures are essential, especially when handling biometric information for the purpose of identification, authentication, or medical analysis. Data protection regulations like

---

[10] ICO—power imbalance https://harperjames.co.uk/news/biometrics-for-employee-monitoring/.

GDPR, CCPA, and regional financial regulatory frameworks require companies to demonstrate their abilities to protect the data they hold to a reasonable standard. Regular security audits and updates are necessary to identify and address potential vulnerabilities, ensuring that biometric data remains secure and private.

Ensure Accuracy

When it comes to false positives and negatives, it's important to continuously monitor the expected quality against a defined benchmark. It's necessary to perform regular updates and rigorous testing of biometric systems to maintain high performance standards. Additionally, efforts to address and prevent biases in biometric systems will ensure fairness and equality across genders and racial differences like skin tone.

Limit to Ethically Defensible Use

Using biometric data responsibly and ethically can limit oneself in what is possible. Just because it can be technically done, doesn't mean it's wise to. Policies must be in place to prevent the use of biometric data for surveillance or discriminatory practices. Biometric systems should be used in ways that respect human rights and freedoms and adhere to ethical standards.

Compliance and Legal Considerations

Ensuring all biometric data practices comply with legal requirements helps mitigate risks. Cooperation with regulatory authorities during investigations or audits is also necessary to maintain compliance and legal integrity.

Traditionally, regulated industries like banks, insurance companies, and healthcare providers had to follow strict data-regulation laws, but a myriad of upcoming privacy regulations worldwide make all organizations large and small accountable for compliance.

Accountability and User Education

Organizations and entities must follow a clear accountability framework for handling biometric data and assigning responsibility to specific individuals or teams. This way, it's clear who has continuous responsibility to maintain the approved and reasonable status quo. They must also educate users about the importance and implications of biometric data security, and provide guidance on protecting their biometric information. Users must be informed about their rights related to biometric data under applicable laws, and mechanisms for addressing and resolving complaints or breaches involving biometric data must be implemented.

Food for thought Can you come up with three ways your organization might assess some of the risks described in this chapter?

Summary

Anytime a decision is made based upon biometrics, there is a small chance of an error. This chapter addresses several consequences of erroneous conclusions. Aside from the inescapable chance of errors, Biometrics presents concerns such as privacy issues and racial bias. Developers of systems utilizing biometric data must consider accessibility for all users and appropriate collection and storage of personal data.

In Chapter 10, we address usability in terms of availability and practicality. The idea of the intent of the user to engage with a device is another important topic in the next chapter.

CHAPTER 10

Usability and Practicality

When looking at the practicality and usability of biometrics in the real world, we encounter limitations and friction that make it more difficult to address the targeted problem. In this chapter, we look into some base-level considerations when designing and implementing a product utilizing biometric data. We begin with a discussion of how workable the product should be in terms of availability, practicality, and usability. Then, we look at the issue of intent—whether the user intends to engage with a system that collects and analyzes their biometric data.

These are two important levels of planning and decision-making that must go into the implementation of a product or service that relies on biometric data to function. Thus, it is essential to include awareness and understanding from the onset of pursuing this type of technological use.

How Usable Is the Product?

When developing a product, it is essential to consider many pragmatic concerns. This section examines a product's availability, practicality, and usability in the early design stages.

CHAPTER 10   USABILITY AND PRACTICALITY

Availability: Do People Have Access to the Technology They Need?

When planning to build a service that solves a problem using biometrics, it's important to assess if people have access to the technology they need to use the service in the intended way. Or equally important is what you intend to offer to people who don't have access to the necessary technology.

The target audience you want to build for has a significant impact on how the people you target gain access to the required technology. Table 10-1 shows three target population segments in terms of access to necessary technology. Differences among these scenarios hinge on who decides which technology end users access. For instance, the smartphone a consumer chooses affects its biometric features. Yet, consumers rarely buy based solely on biometrics. As mentioned earlier, the proportion of devices with biometric capabilities has grown. For services relying on this technology, this proportion is vital for product success.

Table 10-1. *Technology purchase decisions and access to products utilizing biometrics*

Target segment	Examples of services using biometrics	How they make technology purchase decisions	Level of influence on technology decisions
Consumers	Mobile and web-based applications	Largely based on market availability, cost, and how familiar they are with the brands	Very low
Workforce (in your company)	Mobile and web-based applications for use within their work environment	Depending on the maturity of the business, often through centralized IT procurement. Influencing factors are cost and where in the procurement lifecycle you currently are.	Medium-High
Infrastructure	Hardware-based services for shared use like ATMs, gyms, airports, etc.	Usually through projects and longer-term infrastructure investments. Long life cycles can slow down the frequency in which innovation is introduced.	High

When deploying biometrics-based services to consumers or even your workforce, some questions must be considered. First, how many target users have the technology available to support the use of the desired biometric traits? And what is the path to increase this number over time?

Once you understand the gap between how you want people to use your service and who has access to the technology it requires, you must make the hard decision: What must be offered to those who don't have access to adequate technology?

What do you offer to those who can't use the service the way it's intended to be used? There are two main approaches to this problem. Either those people cannot use the service and won't be customers, or an alternative must be provided that removes the requirement of having that specific technology. This often means not using the desired biometric trait.

Addressing the option of simply allowing potential customers to be excluded is outside the scope of this book. That is mainly a commercial question with possible legal implications. We'll focus on how to find a workaround.

Providing an alternative can be tricky as it potentially undermines the added value of the use of biometrics. Let's use the example of a service that uses fingerprints to make payment approvals, a process that is often in place for payment services and e-commerce applications. When prompting the user to perform a fingerprint scan to authorize a payment, the device will compare the provided fingerprint with a previously created template and assess the likelihood of them matching. The device then will provide this assessment to the application, and the payment request will either be approved or rejected. This provides a high assurance that the transaction has been approved by the person previously designated as the device owner. This is a simplified explanation of the process.

Suppose you have to provide a fallback to people who can't use a fingerprint scanner. In that case, this is an alternative biometric trait like facial recognition using a built-in camera or a knowledge factor like a PIN or password.

Having knowledge factors will open up an attack vector to the service that was intended to be removed. It will make it significantly easier for someone who got their hands on someone's device to authorize payments on their behalf. Building a fallback can be useful for business and regulatory reasons but also introduces complexity that can be harder to maintain.

Practicality

Having access to technology is crucial, but having it at the right time and having it work where and when needed adds significantly more complexity to the question. In this chapter, we're defining practicality by looking at the aspects of environment and connectivity.

Environment

The challenge of biometrics is translating a human's physiological or behavioral characteristics into a digital signal. When acquiring a biometric trait using a sensor, like a camera, fingerprint scanner, or microphone, the environment can significantly impact the quality of the collected data.

Let There Be Light (or Not)

Lighting conditions play an important role in extracting biometric information when visual sensors are used. The example that will likely come to your mind first is facial recognition, which uses a camera to capture a person's image to get the information needed for the facial recognition and identification process.

Resolution, contrast, and color accuracy must meet the standards required by the algorithms used to acquire the quality needed to perform facial recognition.

In controlled environments like security terminals at an airport, the operator of the biometric system can ensure that proper lighting is available to acquire a usable image of the person's face that can be processed for its intended use.

CHAPTER 10   USABILITY AND PRACTICALITY

When building a facial recognition system that runs on consumer devices, including smartphones, computers, and televisions, the lighting conditions will vary significantly, potentially making the acquisition of adequate visual material impossible.

FaceID, the face recognition system introduced by Apple in 2017 that uses an array of front-facing sensors, including but not limited to a camera, to unlock devices and perform other authentication steps, is a good example of such a service. It's unlikely that people only want to unlock their phones in perfect daylight. Situations in which they want to do this in the dark or with significant light coming in from the back or side are common and need to be addressed. Apple addressed this by adding sensors that are less dependent on visible light.

While Apple has control over the hardware platform and can use bespoke sensors in its products to perform face-based biometric measurements, other technology vendors might only have access to a two-dimensional image captured by a camera and, therefore, rely more on their algorithms to extract a usable image.

There are also other biometric use cases where light plays a crucial role. Fitness Trackers that measure our heart rate or oxygen saturation in our blood use LED (Light Emitting Diodes) that analyze the reflection of the light to extract the biometric signal. Any light coming from outside that overlaps the spectrum of the LED light can impact the collected data and lead to inaccurate results.

Noise

When microphones perform a biometric test based on a person's voice, the noise levels around them can be critical. When building a service that verifies a customer's identity using their voice before they get to talk to a customer care representative on the phone, the voice acquisition is unlikely to work properly when the customer is at a rock concert. While this might be an unusual situation for someone to check the balance of their retirement account, it's more realistic that they would have to do it in a room with other people or while commuting from/to work.

When deploying such a service, it's important to define the level and type of noise that is unacceptable. This decision is far from technical, but it also impacts the rest of the business, and clarity over these limitations is important.

Clothing

Everyone who lives in a climate with distinct seasons experiences the problem of unlocking their smartphones during the cold winter months. In these months, people are more likely to wear gloves covering their fingertips or scarves blocking their faces when being outdoors. While these items of clothing meant to keep us warm can be temporarily removed, there are other situations where this is not feasible.

If you want to deploy a biometric system that will be used by people who are required to wear protective gear, like gloves, face masks, and helmets, the acquisition of the biometric trait might become impossible, and even though they have the right technology available to them, the use becomes impracticable.

Did You Know?

At the beginning of the COVID-19 pandemic, it became clear how often we used our faces to unlock a device or authorize a transaction. When people started wearing masks, the acquisition of face information was disrupted.

Apple had to devise a workaround to make FaceID work for people wearing masks. So, they released an update that would allow users to change the settings on their phones so they could unlock their phones when wearing masks. This feature would only work for iPhones running a specific version of their operating system or higher. The accuracy of the process is expected to go down as the available information to perform facial recognition is limited by the presence of a mask. There are no numbers available from Apple that describe the level of accuracy loss when wearing a face mask.

Usability

The final element is usability. Do people understand how to properly use the technology given to them? Do people feel confident in using it and trust that it works accurately?

When engaging with any digital surface, people need to know what is expected of them and how to perform a specific task. The experience often starts before the person approaches the devices because that's when they form the intent of doing something.

Every Terminal Is Different

If you have experienced approaching a ticket machine in a train station in a foreign city or country, you can relate to this. Past experience, or the lack thereof, puts many of us under stress. Having to perform an unknown task to achieve the known outcome of having a valid ticket to reach the destination can lead to anxiety and uncertainty before even approaching the ticket machine.

This stress doesn't come from nowhere. It comes from a gained experience that these ticket terminals are all different, and there's always a steep learning curve when getting a train ticket at a type of terminal that is new to us.

Dario has lived much of his life in Switzerland, the country of trains. Multiple generations of ticket machines often are seen in the same region, sometimes even the same train station. With fewer train stations offering points of sale where a ticket can be bought from a person, people are forced to use these machines.

Ticket machines at train stations are by far not the only type of terminal we have to interact with regularly. There are payment terminals, where the place to insert the card varies from model to model, and, of course, the ATM (Automated Teller Machine) to withdraw cash.

What does this have to do with biometrics? The types of terminals mentioned earlier are places where we'll see increased use of biometric traits to make these transactions more secure. If the consistency of experience doesn't improve, we will encounter an even broader variety of usability patterns.

In summary, it's important to understand that replacing the status quo—for example, a PIN—with something "better and stronger" is rarely as straightforward as it seems. While using a fingerprint is more secure than a four-to-six-digit numeric code, it can't be easily replaced.

Using Common User Experience Patterns

People familiar with the Apple ecosystem know the value of standardized and commonly used user experiences. At least for services that use the device capabilities known as TouchID or FaceID to verify that you're the legitimate owner of a device, the experience is very consistent. Whenever you perform an authentication (login) or approve a payment, the device asks you to perform a biometric check with a fallback of using a numeric PIN.

There's a variety of advantages that come when commonly used modules for the user experience can be used:

- **Learning curve**: People don't have to learn a new behavior for every service they use. Using recognizable elements allows them to build on past learned interactions.

- **Trust**: Predictable and known interaction elements also build trust. While people might now know who is behind the newest app they just installed, they have an existing trust relationship with the company that built their phone or the operating system that runs on it. Bad actors often try to build on said trust and create the perception that the victim of an attack is interacting with a trusted brand.

- **Easier to implement**: For developers building new services and apps, using commonly used elements to offer the desired functionality and user experience can significantly reduce the development effort. For most companies, creating their own biometric system is not a part of their core competence.

Platform vendors like Google and Microsoft also use this approach to make user experiences more familiar.

Example Scenario: Replace a PIN with a Fingerprint

When we want to withdraw money from an ATM, we use our physical card as a possession factor (something we own) and the PIN as the knowledge factor (something we know) to prove that we're the legitimate person to withdraw money from a specific bank account.

Like any other knowledge factor, a PIN can be stolen or guessed by a malicious attacker. If said knowledge factor can be replaced by an inheritance factor (Something we are) like a fingerprint, then this type of attack vector can be mitigated.

If ATM vendors decide to install fingerprint sensors in their machines to allow banks to request the customer to perform a biometric authentication instead of typing the PIN, then this would change the usability of said ATM. Each of these vendors would have to make a series of decisions that would impact the technical design and usability of their products:

- Where should the Fingerprint sensor be placed? It must be accessible to all users and protected from the elements, such as wind or rain.

- How do you explain to people how to use the fingerprint sensor? Using a new authentication factor will come as a surprise and potentially throw them off. Usability also means preventing potential negative consequences of asking people to change how they do something they have done many times before.

When designing a completely new ATM model, these types of usability decisions can be made with the new method in focus. Replacing all terminals might not be economically viable, so banks will push vendors to upgrade and retrofit existing models. This will impose several restrictions on the product design team as they need to work around the ATM's existing design and architecture.

Intent

It is crucial to consider the intent of the person whose biometric data is being utilized. A separate concern from consent, intent can have a little more play. In designing a system using people's biometric signals, the product must be calibrated for a level of interest to engage.

Showing and Detecting Intent

Human-to-human interaction is deeply engraved into our lives. When interacting with people, we have established patterns to show intent of engaging with each other. Some can be culturally specific, but we mostly follow similar patterns. When you're in a room with multiple people and want to address a specific person, you're likely to call their name and look for eye contact to signal intent to communicate.

In this context, we're defining intent as a signal of desire and awareness for a human to engage with a biometric system. Intent can be compared to the beginning to establish a social contract between the human carrying the biometric traits and the machine consuming them. From a system design perspective, there are two sides of the coin:

1. **Show intent**: How does the person show intent to engage with a system that wants to (start to) collect biometric information?

2. **Detect intent**: How does the system detect if and when the person has shown the intent to provide biometric information?

The process of showing and detecting intent can differ based on various factors, such as the biometric trait(s) being utilized, how they're being collected, and the relationship between the carrier of the biometric trait and the collection sensor.

Unlocking a Smartphone

Interaction with devices can work similarly but differ in some areas. One of the acts of presenting intent to a digital device most often is unlocking a smartphone. If our phone uses a fingerprint sensor to identify us, our intent is picking up the phone and putting our finger onto the fingerprint sensor. When picking up the phone, a gyroscope detects a change in the orientation and movement of the device. This registers some level of intent to use the phone. When placing the finger on the fingerprint sensor, the sensor detects the presence of an object that could be a finger. This act is a second expression of intent to use and open the device.

When unlocking a phone with face recognition, showing and detecting intent is a similar procedure—starting with picking up the device and then engaging with the mobile device's front-facing camera. As with the preceding fingerprint example, the gyroscope first detects a change in orientation. But this time, the second indication of intent is when we look at the front-facing camera. The sensor attempts to identify a face and assess if the face is pointing at the camera and if the eyes are open. The camera starts collecting continuous images and evaluates if the person is aware and looking at the camera.

Approving a Payment

Regulatory requirements such as PSD2 in the European Union require providers of electronic payment services to include strong customer authentication to keep financial fraud within defined thresholds.

This means that when a payment is initiated, the process must involve at least two independent authentication factors, categorized as knowledge factor (something only the user knows), possession (something only the user possesses), and inherence (something the user is).

Biometric authentication, falling under the category of inherence, is increasingly being utilized in this context. By leveraging unique physical characteristics such as fingerprints, facial recognition, or iris scans, biometric authentication ensures higher security. This method provides a seamless and user-friendly experience and significantly reduces the risk of unauthorized access. Integrating biometrics into payment approval processes under PSD2 regulation reflects an advanced approach to securing transactions, aligning with the directive's objective of enhancing consumer protection while fostering an innovative and competitive payments environment.

Difficulty of Showing and Assessing Intent

What does it mean when biometric systems don't assess intent by the people they collect data about? Aside from potential legal consequences, which we're not addressing in this part of the book, there are implications for the user experience and even the security of a product using biometric signals.

CHAPTER 10   USABILITY AND PRACTICALITY

Let's start with a couple of examples where the lack of intent detection could lead to confusion or unwanted effects for a product. These examples are relatively generic. Different vendors of such products might address these risks in different ways.

Home Assistants with Displays

In recent years, companies like Amazon and Google have launched a variety of devices that combine small screens with voice-powered assistants. These screens are built to show information in a visual way, like the owner's calendar, shopping list, pictures, and videos. In contrast to smartphones, these devices are stationary—often in rooms where multiple people are present.

If such a device uses a built-in camera to identify the person to show contextualized and personalized information, not checking for intent can lead to a confusing user experience and potentially reveal private information to someone else.

Terminals with Face Recognition in Public Places

The use of facial recognition in public places like airports is growing. When entering countries like the United States, the United Kingdom, Japan, and others, facial recognition has become crucial to making travel faster and cheaper.

Some terminals are built to control the flow of passengers so that the person standing in front of the camera is aware and has started to engage with the system while approaching it. This can be seen as a way of guiding the passenger to show intent and making it easier for the system to detect it.

The process of using face-recognition to facilitate border-crossing checks at airports can be split into two parts:

- **Part 1:** Scan the passport to let the passenger through the first gate. This step assesses the identity the passenger uses to enter the country. From a usability perspective, it is also a way to control the flow of passengers getting to the next stage, where a camera is positioned.

- **Part 2:** Face recognition. At this point, the passenger is prompted to stand on a dedicated spot, illustrated by the yellow footprint on the floor. This ensures that the person is in the camera's view area. The passenger, by standing on the designated spot and seeing their face—as captured by the camera—on the screen, is aware that they are using a facial recognition system.

This is a good example of how physical and visual cues are used to gather intent when performing facial recognition. Examples where the terminals are just "free-standing" can negatively impact perceived and real intent collection.

Lack of Intent

In many situations, intent can't be assessed in the process, and biometric data is being collected without the person's explicit intent and awareness.

CCTV surveillance cameras or smart doorbells with cameras are good examples of systems that gather biometric traits—faces—without having the person actively engage with them. They focus more on gathering information about faces within their field of view. The lack of intent is often accepted here as no direct transaction of information automatically results from it. If the smart doorbell would unlock the door when a family member appears on the camera, collecting intent to enter the door would be an essential check to protect the door from being unlocked just when the person walks by.

CHAPTER 10   USABILITY AND PRACTICALITY

Reasonable Expectations

Whenever people approach or see a device that can act as a sensor of biometric information, they have expectations about how it works. Given the likelihood that we're not encountering these devices for the first time, our expectations have been shaped by previous experiences. Here are some examples of areas where past experiences can define expectations:

- **Security Cameras** have been around for decades. They are usually installed in public places or businesses. When seeing such a camera, most people expect these cameras to record video footage (with or without audio) and delete it after a defined period unless an incident is reported. Part of the video footage is analyzed and used to file charges or run investigations by law enforcement or the authority that installed the camera. This is how security cameras have worked over the past decades, shaping our understanding and creating what we're calling reasonable expectations.

- **Fingerprint Scanners to Enter Buildings**: Buildings with restricted access, like Data centers housing IT Infrastructure, sometimes have a fingerprint sensor that checks if the person attempting to enter matches the list of authorized people. This expectation has been explicitly or implicitly created in the past.

- **My Voice is My Password**. Customers must use a common phrase when calling their bank, insurance, or financial advisor. Over the years, the expectation has developed that this voiceprint is compared to a previously enrolled template.

These are just three examples of situations where people's biometric traits are being collected, and people's past experiences have defined what they expect to happen in the background.

These expectations might vary depending on the person, but if they are generally aligned with each other, they can be designated to be "reasonable."

If the security camera now doesn't just record the video data for a specific period but performs facial and voice recognition against a set of templates like a criminal database or customer database to inform law enforcement or create movement profiles across locations covered by multiple cameras, this would conflict with the expectations people captured by the camera have come to get used to.

If the fingerprint scanner compared the print provided to enter the building and automatically performed a scan with a database of fingerprint templates found at crime scenes, this would not align with the person's expectations.

If the bank using its customers' voices to assess their identity would analyze the voice to detect Alzheimer's or dementia, this would also break reasonable expectations.

While these are certainly extreme examples that could result in legal liability, they're meant to show that there can be a significant gap between what people expect to happen with their biometrics and what technically would be possible. If Kellogg's decides to increase the sugar level in its cereal, it must change the label on its packaging. If a dumb security camera suddenly becomes smart, this is unclear to people in the sensor's field of view.

When building systems that collect biometric information, it's important to understand what reasonable expectations people will have. Gaps between these expectations and the reality of how the product functions must be carefully considered and communicated.

CHAPTER 10 USABILITY AND PRACTICALITY

Summary

The functionality of a biometric system is built on its availability, practicality, and usability. The device used, users' individuality, and previous user experience all contribute to the functionality of a product or procedure utilizing biometric data. Beyond functionality questions, due consideration must be given to a customer's intent to use a product.

Availability of a product is just the base of the pyramid. If a bank wants its customers to use facial recognition to log in to their app, customers will need devices with adequate front-facing cameras. People need to open their phones at various light levels or access accounts using voice recognition, even in noisy places. A product must function in the real world, which is messy. Beyond functioning smoothly, a product should also promote trust and confidence with users.

Conclusion

Thank you for reading our book. Our goal has been to provide a comprehensive understanding of biometrics, from the various types of biometrics to the risks and responsibilities that come with using biometrics in modern technology. Exploring both the promise and the challenges of biometric systems, this book has equipped you with the knowledge to navigate this complex field with more confidence.

Laying the Foundation

Part 1 provided the foundational knowledge to understand the evolution of using biometric traits for identification and other applications, starting with a historical overview of the use of biometric data and the driving factors behind it becoming as ubiquitous and omnipresent as it is today.

Next we laid out the terminology and the type of problems that are being solved with the use of biometrics. The questions "Are you real?", "Who are you?", and "How are you?" being the guiding elements.

Further we covered some basic elements of the adversarial behavior most biometric systems eventually face and how they can be addressed with principles like liveness checks.

Sources of Biometrics

In the second part of the book, we discussed a selection of biometric traits and how they can be used to solve desired problems. We both covered the foundations of physiological biometric traits that describe characteristics of our bodies and behavioral traits that reflect how we use our body. By digging deeper into Face and Voice, we provided more insights into how they work and where they're used.

Critical Analysis

The final part of the book facilitates a critical analysis of the field. We believe that providing a mental model to assess the accuracy of the data used to draw further conclusions is crucial in positioning biometric technology correctly.

We dedicated a chapter to risks and responsibilities. The chapter provided you with a generic overview of what limitations need to be considered and what responsibilities need to be addressed when collecting and using biometric data.

The last chapter, diving into practicality and usability, is meant to give you some food for thought on how the use of biometric is and isn't practical in specific situations. Concepts such as Intent declaration and reasonable expectations are part of this last chapter.

Implications and Recommendations

If you're involved in building products and services that use biometrics, you'll need to stay abreast of technological advancements and regulatory changes. Depending on your role, you may rely on a broad range of knowledge coming from specialists in law, technology, and ethics. Don't assume that this or any book will give you a playbook to do it all. Biometrics are a good example of how technology should be understood from many different perspectives.

Closing Remarks

Biometrics play a crucial role in our increasingly digital world, offering both immense potential and significant challenges. As this space continues to innovate and these technologies find their way into our daily lives, it is essential to do so responsibly and ethically. By staying informed and engaged with the evolving landscape of biometrics, we can harness their power to create a safer, more inclusive future for everyone.

Index

A

Accessibility, 94, 135–136, 140
Accuracy, 76, 110–112, 139
Accurate gait extraction, 86
Active liveness, 48, 49
Adermatoglyphia, 59
Artificial intelligence (AI), 35, 40, 73, 101, 104, 120
Athletic training, 87
Attacks
    AI, 40
    vs. biometric signals
        artificially created information, 42
        future threats, 42
        stolen biometric data, 41
    brute force, 39
    defense
        layered approach, 43
        liveness, 43, 44
    mimicry, 40
    phishing, 39
    replay, 39
    spoofing, 39
    synthetic biometrics, 39
    tampering, 40
    templates, 40
Automated fingerprint identification system (AFIS), 9
Automated Teller Machine (ATM), 143, 149–151
Automated voice recognition systems, 103

B

Bad actions
    attacks, 37
    equipment, 38
    expensive, 38
    expertise, 38
    time, 38
Behavioral biometrics, 28, 29, 35, 80, 84, 89–91
Biometric data, 17–19, 21–23, 31, 39, 41, 72, 112, 117, 125, 134, 140, 155
Biometrics
    1850, 8
    1870, 8
    1903, 8
    1904, 8
    1970, 9
    1996, 9

INDEX

Biometrics (*cont.*)
   2001, 9
   2013, 10
   2015, 10
   2017, 10
   accountability, 140
   accuracy, 139
   consent and
      transparency, 138
   early historical use, 6, 7
   environment
      clothing, 147
      FaceID, 147
      lighting conditions, 145
      noise, 146
   ethical standards, 139
   intent
      approving payment, 153
      assess, 153
      detect, 151
      expectations, 156, 157
      facial recognition, public place, 154
      home assistants, 154
      lack, 155
      unlocking a phone, 152
   laptops, 14
   legal and regulatory risks, 136
   legal requirements, 139
   negative consequences, 137
   personal devices/home, 11
   practicality, 145
   privacy concerns, 128, 129
   public spaces, 11
   racial bias, 131
   recent historical use, 7
   security audits, 139
   technology, 143, 144
   usability
      PIN with fingerprint, 150
      ticket machines, 149
      user experience, 149, 150
   uses, 21
Biometric signals
   action, 35
   adaptation, 35
   vs. attacks, 41
   characteristics, 31
   data storage, 33
   decision-making, 35
   FAR/FRR, 35
   high-level steps, 31
   human voice, 32
   machine learning/AI, 35
   many to one matching, 26
   methods, 33
   one to many matching, 26
   one to one matching, 26
   reading, 30
   threshold setting, 35
Biometric traits, 22, 23, 28, 47, 89, 90, 105
   medical purpose, 28
   sentiments, 29
Broadband, 19
Built-in cameras, 17

INDEX

C

Capacitive scanners, 58
CCTV cameras, 12, 25
Cellular data standards, 19
Clearview, 75–77
Client-side facial recognition, 71
Concept drift
    definition, 90
    long-term shift, 90
    short-term shift, 90
Confidence intervals, 127
Consequences of errors
    accountability, 125
    decision analysis/decision trees, 126
    FMEA, 126
    harm to individuals, 125
    judicial proceedings, 125
    monetary impact, 125
    Monte Carlo simulations, 127
    privacy breaches, 125
    Scenario planning, 127
    statistics, 127
Continuous authentication, 82, 87–89
Correctness of measurements
    accuracy, 110
    precision, 110
    reliability, 111
    robustness, 112
    validity, 111

D

Deep learning methods, 34
Deoxyribonucleic acid (DNA)
    characteristics, 64
    databases, 66
    data points, 64
    forensic, 65
    healthcare, 65
    methods, 65
    red blood cells, 65
Detect intent, 152

E

E-commerce applications, 144
Electronic eye-scanning system, 5
Embeddings, 33
Eye tracking, 88

F

Face detection, 70, 71
FaceID, 10, 14, 68, 146, 147, 149
Face recognition, 10, 60, 70, 90, 120, 146, 154–155
Face-search engines, 75–77
Facial analysis
    Amazon's X-Ray feature, 68
    face detection, 70
    face recognition, 70
    features, 67
    home security, 69

Facial analysis (*cont.*)
    identification/authentication, 68
    non-invasive nature, 68
    surveillance systems, 69
    2D *vs.* 3D, 70
Facial recognition, 4, 5, 24
    challenges, 74
    client-side/server-side, 71
    developer integration, 71
    strengths
        comprehensive data points, 72
        front-facing cameras, 72
        non-invasive, 73
        technological advancements, 72
        user familiarity, 73
    weakness
        AI, 73
        diversity/bias issues, 73
        lack of secrecy, 73
Failure Modes and Effects Analysis (FMEA), 126
False acceptance rate (FAR), 35, 125
False negative, 30, 34, 82, 113, 116
False positive, 30, 34, 76, 113, 116, 125, 139
False Rejection Rate (FRR), 35
Feature matching, 34
FIDO Alliance, 136
Fingerprint analysis, 4, 119
Fingerprints
    benefits, 54
    drawbacks, 55, 56
    identify people, 57
    influencing factors, 54
    patterns, 54
    scanners, 57
    unlock devices, 56
Fingerprint scanners, 26, 57, 58, 117, 145, 156
Fingerprint sensors, 10, 14, 17, 56, 150–152
Fitness trackers, 11, 14, 27, 146
Forensics, 64, 118
Front-facing camera, 24, 72, 152, 153

G

Gait analysis
    athletic training, 87
    medical diagnostics, 87
    security and surveillance, 87
Gait recognition, 84–87, 91
Genealogy tests, 65
General Data Protection Regulation (GDPR), 16, 134, 138, 139
Genetic markers, 28

H

Hand movement, 88
Home security systems, 11, 69
Human-to-human interaction, 151

INDEX

I, J, K

Image search, 74, 75
Information Commissioner Office (ICO), 138
International Association of Privacy Professionals (IAPP), 128
Iridology, 61
Iris
    characteristics, 60
    constituents, 59
    uses, 60
    working, 60
Iris pigment epithelium, 59

L

Light Emitting Diodes (LED), 146
Liveness, 29, 43–50
Liveness test, 44

M

Machine learning (ML), 34, 35, 40, 100, 133
Medical diagnostics, 87
Minutiae matching, 33
Monte Carlo simulations, 127
Mouse dynamics, 88
Multimodal liveness, 46, 47

N

Neural networks, 34

O

One to one matching, 25
Optical scanners, 57

P, Q

Passive liveness, 47, 49–50
Pattern matching, 34
Performance of biometrics
    difficulty of computing, 118
    facial recognition, 120
    fingerprints, 118, 119
    layers of quality, 117
    voice recognition, 119, 120
Personal devices, 11, 14–15, 56, 57
Precision, 30, 86, 110–112, 121
Prevalent trait, 91

R

Racial bias
    consent, 134
    legacy of discrimination, 132
    training data, 133
Reliability, 72–74, 86, 110–112, 127
Retina
    characteristics, 62
    scanners, 5, 63
Robustness, 35, 110, 112, 119

S

Scenario planning, 127
Security cameras, 69, 156, 157
Selfie-matching, 24

INDEX

Sensitivity, 112–116, 121
Sensors
    connectivity, 18
    data collection, 18
    facial recognition, 18
    fingerprint, 17
Sentiment analysis, 22, 29, 82, 99
Server-side facial
        recognition, 71, 72
Show intent, 151, 152, 154
Situational
        compartmentalization, 130
SMARTCOPE, 89
Smart devices, 16–17
Smart speakers, 11, 16, 97, 98,
        100, 101
Specificity, 112, 114–116
Statistical/probabilistic
        matching, 34
Statistical significance tests, 127
Stroma, 59
Surveillance, 69, 87, 125, 129, 130,
        133, 139
Surveillance cameras, 12, 13, 87,
        125, 155
Swipe patterns, 88, 89

T

Template matching, 34
Traits, 13, 22–24, 40–42, 45, 67, 79,
        125, 143, 155, 160
2D images, 45, 70, 120

Type I error, 114–116
Type II error, 114–116
TypingDNA, 81
Typing patterns
    authentication at login time, 81
    continuous authentication, 82
    legal risk, 83
    limitations, 82, 83
    privacy, 83
    sentiment analysis, 82
    working, 81

U

Ultrasonic scanners, 58
Unimodal liveness, 46–47

V

Validity, 110–112
Video-enabled doorbells, 3,
        15, 16, 45
Voice-based biometrics, 93
    AI, 104
    capturing, 95
    disadvantages, 95
    early disease detection, 99
    environmental factors, 102, 103
    inheritance factors, 94
    password, 98
    personal assistants, 97
    preventing misuse, 104
    relative stability, 94

replay attacks, 104
sentiment analysis, 99
smart speakers, 97
strengths
    behavioral in nature, 96
    intrinsic characteristic, 96
    medical insights, 96
    natural/intuitive interaction, 96
    technological availability, 96
weakness
    digital misuse, 97
    public exposure, 96
    variability/aging, 97
Voice identification, 5, 25

W, X, Y, Z

Walking patterns
    characteristics, 84
    limitations, 86
Wearable devices, 14, 15
Web Content Accessibility Guidelines (WCAG), 135
Wireless transport, 19
Writing pattern
    dwell time, 80
    error patterns, 80
    flight time, 80
    press-release timing, 80
    pressure sensitivity, 81
    typing rhythm, 81
    typing speed, 80

MIX
Papier aus verantwortungsvollen Quellen
Paper from responsible sources
FSC® C105338

If you have any concerns about our products,
you can contact us on
ProductSafety@springernature.com

In case Publisher is established outside the EU,
the EU authorized representative is:
**Springer Nature Customer Service Center GmbH
Europaplatz 3, 69115 Heidelberg, Germany**

Printed by Libri Plureos GmbH
in Hamburg, Germany